Septuagint: Psalms and the Prayer of Manasseh

Septuagint, Volume 15

SCRIPTURAL RESEARCH INSTITUTE
Published by Digital Ink Productions, 2024

Copyright

Septuagint: Psalms and the Prayer of Manasseh

Second edition. November 15, 2024

Copyright © 2024 Scriptural Research Institute.

ISBN: 978-1-998636-05-1

The Septuagint was translated into Greek at the Library of Alexandria between 250 and 132 BC.

This English translation was created by the Scriptural Research Institute in 2020 through 2024, primarily from the Codex Vaticanus and Codex Alexandrinus, although other Septuagint codice were also used for reference. Additionally, the Aleppo Codex, Leningrad Codex, and the Dead Sea Scrolls were used for comparative analysis.

The image used for the cover is "King David Playing the Harp" by Gerard van Honthorst, painted in 1622.

Table of Contents

TABLE OF CONTENTS

TABLE OF CONTENTS

TABLE OF CONTENTS

TABLE OF CONTENTS

TABLE OF CONTENTS

TABLE OF CONTENTS

TABLE OF CONTENTS

TABLE OF CONTENTS

Forward

In the mid-3rd century BC, King Ptolemy II Philadel-phus of Egypt ordered a translation of the ancient Israelite scriptures for the Library of Alexandria, which resulted in the creation of the Septuagint. The original version, published circa 250 BC, only included the Torah, or in Greek terms, the Pentateuch. The Torah is the five books traditionally credited to Moses, circa 1500 BC: Cosmic Genesis, Exodus, Leviticus, Numbers, and Deuteronomy. According to Jewish tradition, the orig-inal Torah was lost when the Babylonians destroyed the Temple of Solomon and was later rewritten by Ezra the Scribe from memory during the Second Temple period.

It is generally accepted that there were several versions of the ancient Israelite scriptures before the translation of the Septuagint, mostly written in Canaanite or Aramaic, although the older sections of the Torah appear to have originated in Akkadian Cuneiform.

The Psalms are a complex collection of hymns and prayers likely composed over many centuries, and by various authors. The earliest psalms are attributed to King David or are written for King David, including the first 40, which are likely the original group of psalms. Many other psalms are attributed to, or written for Asaph, Solomon, Ethan, Moses, Jeremiah, Haggai, Zachariah, the sons of Korah, or the sons of Jehonadab.

FORWARD

Some of the psalms have internal historical references that indicate the likely time frame in which they were written. King David is generally believed to have lived around 1000 BC by those who accept him as a historical figure, and Asaph, Solomon, and Ethan all lived around the same time, so those who accept the Psalms as having been written by authors that they are attributed to, would generally place the origin of most of the texts to around 1000 BC. The life of Moses has been dated to anywhere between the 16th and 13th centuries BC, and the original sons of Korah lived at the same time, however, the sons of Korah were also the priests in Solomon's Temple before they were replaced by the Levites. Jehonadab lived during the reign of the Israelite King Jehu, who lived circa 800 BC, while Jeremiah's life is dated to circa 600 BC, and the lives of Haggai and Zachariah are dated to circa 500 BC.

Ignoring the attributions found in the Psalms, some internal references point to specific time periods between 900 and 332 BC for the origin of the Psalms. One of the historical references that appears repeatedly in the Psalms is Egypt as being in the land of Ham. The Hebrew term Ham referred to any black-skinned people, much like the Greek term Aethiopian, and therefore this dates some of the psalms to the Nubian rule of Egypt, between 744 and 656 BC. While the Masoretic Texts, the

Hebrew translation of the Israelite texts refer to the god of the Psalms as Yhŭh (יהוה), Yahweh (יְהֹוָה), or Yehvih (יְהֹוִה), the Septuagint used the translation of cyrios (κύριοσ), meaning lord. This was interpreted as being a later redaction by Christians until corroborating translations were discovered among the Dead Sea Scrolls.

While Yhŭh is found in most of the Dead Sea Scrolls, either in Hebrew (יהוה) or Canaanite (𐤉𐤄𐤅𐤄), some Dead Sea Scrolls also include the translation of "my Lord" (אדני), where the Septuagint has "the lord" (ὁ κύριοσ). The Septuagint also includes the translation of Lord Lord (κύριε κύριε), where the Masoretic texts has Lord Yhŭh (אדני יהוה), Lord Yehvih (אֲדֹנָי יְהֹוִה), or Yehvah Lord (יְהֹוָה אֲדֹנָיֿ), confirming the Hebrew translations were not consistent. The Greeks did translate Yhŭh from the Aramaic Yhŭ (𐤉𐤄𐤅) as Iaw (Ιαω) in some of the books of the Septuagint, however, there is no evidence of Iaw being in Psalms before Simon's Hebrew translation.

The earliest references to the Septuagint's Lord in the Psalms, treat the Lord as the Sun or refer to the Lord as living in the Sun. In the later psalms, the sun was a completely separate object from the Lord, which is consistent with the changing religion of the region recorded in both the Israelite and Judahite books of the Kingdoms and the archaeological record. 4th Kingdoms

(Masoretic Kings) describes King Josiah's reforms circa 625 BC. From 4ᵗʰ Kingdoms chapter 23:

> The king commanded Hilkiah the high priest, and the priests of the second order, and them that kept the door, to bring out of the temple of the Lord all the vessels that were made for Ba'al, and for Asherah, and all the army of Shamayim, and he burnt them outside of Jerusalem in the fields of Kidron, and took the ashes of them to the Temple of El. He burnt the sacred male prostitutes, who the kings of Judah had appointed, and those burnt incense in the Bamahs and in the cities of Judah, and the places around Jerusalem, and those that burnt incense to Ba'al, Shemesh, Yarikh, the Zodiac, and the power of the armies of Shamayim.

> He carried out the Asherah from the Temple of the Lord to the brook Kidron, and burnt it at the brook Kidron, and ground it to powder, and threw its powder on the sepulchers of the sons of the people. He pulled down the Palace of Qetesh that were by the Temple of the Lord, where the women wove tents for the Asherah. He brought up all the priests from the cities of Judah and defiled the Bamahs where the priests burnt incense, from Geba even to Beersheba.

> He pulled down the house of the gates that were by the door of the gate of Joshua the ruler of the city, on a man's left hand at the gate of the city. The priests of the Bamahs did not go up to the altar of the Lord in Jerusalem, and they only ate leavened bread among their brothers. He defiled

Tafeth which is in the valley of the son of Hinnom, constructed for a man to cause his son or his daughter to pass through the fire to Moloch. He burnt the horses which the king of Judah had given to Shemesh in the entrance of the Temple of the Lord, by the treasury of Nathan the king's eunuch, in the suburbs, and he burnt the Chariot of Shemesh with fire.

Shemesh was the Canaanite god of the sun, who was essentially the same as the Greek Helios before Josiah's reforms. Like Helios, Shemesh rode on a chariot pulled by four flying horses. The four horses are a reference to what are commonly called sundogs today, the refracted light that appears 22° to the left and right of the Sun, and in rare cases again at 44° when there are ice crystals in the atmosphere. The Psalms include many references to the Lord shining down from the sky, and the name of the Lord enduring as long as the sun. Psalms 18 claims that the Lord lives in the sun, suggesting he was something other than the sun, even in the early Psalms.

In the sun he is accustomed to living, and he comes out like a bridegroom out of his chamber. He will celebrate as the giant running his course. His going out is from the extremity of the sky, and his circuit to the other end of the sky, and no one will be hidden from his heat.

This idea that the Lord lived in the sun, may connect the early Israelite religion to the cults of Aten and Atum in Egypt, who were also considered to be solar manifestations. Aten was the solar god of Egypt during the New Kingdom era reforms of Pharaoh Akhenaten during the mid-1300s BC and mentioned in the Song of Deborah in the Book of Judges from the same era. Tm ($\rightleftharpoons$), generally anglicized as Atum, was the solar god of the city of Iůnŭ ($\overset{\circ}{l}\,\circled8$) during the Egyptian Second Intermediate Period, when the Septuagint's dating placed Moses' exodus from Egypt. Iůnŭ was later called Aven (אֶוֶן) by the Israelites, based on the New Kingdom pronunciation of ʔaːnə, Heliopolis (Ἡλίου πόλις), meaning "sun city" by the Greeks, and Ôn (Ⲱⲛ) by the Coptic Egyptians. Atum's wife was Hathor ($\boxtimes\mathring{\mathfrak{m}}$) during the Middle Kingdom, who was also known as the "Lady of the Offerings," and "She who grows what she becomes." These titles began being worshiped as separate goddesses after the fall of the Middle Kingdom, and by the New Kingdom were generally considered different, but ill-defined goddesses. Atum's son in Iůnŭ was Iôḥŭ ($\text{⌐}\,\_\,\text{⌐}\,\text{⌐}\,\text{⌐}\,\blacktriangleright$), the moon god. During the New Kingdom Era, when Canaan was part of the Egyptian Empire, this trinity was incorporated into the Canaanite religion and formed the trinity worshiped at Baalbek. Baalbek was also known as Heliopolis by the Greeks, as the ancient Ba'al that was worshiped there was a solar god. By the Roman era, he was associated with Jove, and no longer associated with the sun, which appears to be the same transition that the Ba'al of Jerusalem underwent during the era.

Atum's wife was also known as the "hand of Atum," and a similar term, the "hand of the Lord" is used throughout the book of Psalms, which suggests the term found in the Israelite books was translated from Egyptian texts. At Baalbek, Ba'al's wife was known as Astarte, the Phoenician version of the goddess the Israelites and Judahites called Asherah. Asherah was one of the deities banned under the rule of King Josiah in circa 625 BC, and worshiped in Solomon's temple alongside Ba'al before the reforms. The son of Ba'al and Astarte at Baalbek was known as Adon, meaning Lord, while the son of Atum and Hathor in On was known as Îôhŭ, which is likely the origin of the Canaanite name Yhŭh (AᎽAZ), and the Aramaic name Yhŭ (ᒋᒧ^). The word Îôh (^) was the north Egyptian word for the moon, however, when treated as a god, it was modified to Îôhŭ (ᛁ___ᛁᛟᛉ^ᚥ).

Both the city of Îŭnŭ and the temple of Atum (Per-Atum), are mentioned as places in Egypt associated with the Israelite patriarchs Joseph, Moses, and Aaron, supporting the connection between the trinities of Canaan and Heliopolis. Likewise, Moses created a statue of a bronze serpent, while Aaron created a statue of a golden calf in the story of the Exodus. Which is how

Atum and Îôḥů were traditionally depicted. The bronze serpent was carried with the tabernacle into Canaan, and ultimately erected in the temple of Solomon, where it stood for hundreds of years before King Hezekiah destroyed it during his reforms, as recorded in 4th Kingdoms, chapter 18:

> In the third year of King Hoshea son of Elah of Israel, Hezekiah son of Ahaz king of Judah began to reign. He was twenty-five years old when he began to reign, and he reigned twenty-nine years in Jerusalem. His mother's name was Abi, daughter of Zachariah. He did that which was right in the sight of the Lord, like all that his father David did. He removed the Bamahs and broke in pieces the steles, and completely destroyed Asherah, and the bronze serpent that Moses had made, because until those days the Israelites had burnt incense to it, which he had called Neesthan.

While it is clear that the bronze serpent Neesthan was worshiped at King Solomon's temple, it is not clear that it was the statue of Ba'al that Solomon had erected and Hezekiah removed, however, it would be consistent with the religion followed in Îůnů, where Joseph and Aaron had served as priests. The earliest surviving depictions of the Israelite god Yahweh, from Kuntillet Ajrud in the Sinai desert, which dates to around 900 BC, depict him as a calf and describe him as the calf of Asherah. Therefore, at the time Yhůh was the child of

Ba'al, the Canaanite version of Atum, and Asherah the Canaanite version of Hathor, and depicted as a calf, making him the Canaanite version of Iȯḥu̇, the moon god.

The fact that the early Psalms show a great similarity to the Egyptian religion of northern Egypt, specifically the city of Iu̇nu̇, as well as the Canaanite religion, specifically of the Baalbek region, supports the age of the earliest Psalms as being pre-Josiah, and almost certainly pre-Hezekiah, and therefore earlier than 715 BC. According to all surviving records of David's son Solomon, his first wife was an Egyptian princess, meaning that David's kingdom must have had very close relations with Egypt.

The Prayer of Manasseh was found in some copies of the Septuagint, but not all. It is believed to have been added in the 2nd century BC, which is why it is not found in all copies. The current scholarly view is that it was likely written in Greek, and is not the original Prayer of Manasseh mentioned in the Septuagint's 2nd Paralipomenon, however, translations of the versions found in the Septuagint are the only version found in the various translations of 2nd Paralipomenon, including the Syriac and Ge'ez translations, which supports the version in the Septuagint as being in the Aramaic translations the Greeks translated. Fragments of a different

Prayer of Manasseh have been discovered among the dead sea scrolls, written in Hebrew, which is probably a translation of a Canaanite Prayer of Manasseh. It is unclear which Prayer of Manasseh is the original, and both could be original prayers by Manasseh, who was reported as being a Judahite king from the era when the Judahites were writing in Canaanite, and taken north to Assyria, where Aramaic was the common form of writing. The story of his capture is not corroborated by Assyrian sources, and seems unlikely, leaving the question of where the Aramaic Prayer came from a mystery.

The 5th century Codex Alexandrinus includes the Prayer of Manasseh as one of the 14 Odes, appearing directly after Psalms, however, it often appears at different positions within Bibles and is treated as a separate work by many Christian denominations. Jerome's Vulgate, the 4th century Latin translation of the Bible, included the Prayer of Manasseh at the end of 2nd Chronicles (2nd Paralipomenon), where it also appears in the Ge'ez translation. In addition to the Greek translation, ancient copies survive in Armenian, Latin, Ge'ez, Old Slavonic, and Syriac, all of which are translations of the Septuagint's version, and not the version found among the Dead Sea Scrolls.

The Prayer of Manasseh is unusual in that it is written by one of the 'evil' kings of Judea, who restored

Baalism, and restored the statue of Ba'al to King Solomon's Temple. It is a prayer dedicated to 'the Lord' which is a direct translation of the title Ba'al and may, therefore, be seen as a Baalist prayer. This is something that has concerned Jews and Christians throughout history, which is why it is not universally considered canon by either Jews or Christians.

The author of the Septuagint's 2nd Paralipomenon (Masoretic Divrei-hayyamim) attempted to resolve the question of Manasseh's prayer by adding a story of his repentance and return to worshiping the Lord after being imprisoned by the King of Assyria, however, that story is not viewed as possible by many, as it would have meant that Judea was conquered by the Assyrians, who then incarcerated the Judean King in Nineveh. There are no records of this, however, Manasseh is mentioned as the King of Judea in the Assyrian records, and the two nations appear to have had cordial relations. The fact that the author of 2nd Paralipomenon felt he needed to explain the existence of the Prayer of Manasseh, proves it was in use by Jews at the time, although, it may not be the Prayer that ended up in the Septuagint. Fragments of a Hebrew Prayer of Manasseh have been found among the Dead Sea Scrolls, however, not enough of them survive to determine how much the two Prayers originally deviated.

In 200 BC, the Greek Kingdom of Syria under the Seleucid Dynasty took Judea from Egypt and began an effort to Hellenize the Judeans, which included erecting a statue of Zeus in the Second Temple in Jerusalem and effectively banning traditional Judaism. This Hellenizing activity was partially successful, creating the Sadducee faction of Judaism, however, it also led to the Maccabean Revolt in 165 BC, which itself created the independent Kingdom of Judea. This Kingdom had a tenuous alliance with the Roman Republic until General Pompey conquered Syria into the Roman Republic in 69 BC. Pompey's goal was to liberate Greek-speaking communities in the Middle East that had fallen under the rule of non-Greeks when the Seleucids Syrian Empire had collapsed, and he carved up Judea, and Edom to the southeast, placing Greek-speaking cities under the protection of the Roman province of Syria. He also liberated several smaller communities that had been occupied by Judea, granting them self-government, including Ashdod, Yavne, Jaffa, Dora, Marissa, and Samaria.

A series of wars including both Julius Caesar's campaigns, and a Parthian invasion led to the weakening of the Hasmonean dynasty, and in 37 AD, the Roman Senate appointed the Edomite king Herod the Great as king of Judea. Herod's rule wasn't particularly popular, as he allowed the Romans to establish themselves within

Judea, however, he did expand Judea, reintegrating the Greek and Samaritan cities, and annexing Galilee and Edom. When he died, his kingdom was divided between four successors, a situation that ended in 66 AD when the Romans conquered the region. An uprising in 120 AD led to the Jews being exiled from Judea, and the region became a Greco-Roman colony. In the wake of the Jews, the Samaritans rose in numbers, along with the Christians once Christianity was legalized. Between 529 and 555 AD, the Samaritans revolted and were effectively annihilated, by Constantinople the Eastern Roman capital.

Outside of Judea, the Septuagint was the dominant form of Jewish scriptures across the Greek-speaking world, which by the beginning of the Christian era extended from the Roman Empire in the west, to the Indo-Greek Kingdom in the east. Jewish traders had established small colonies along the trade routes of the Red Sea and the Indian Ocean, reaching as far south as Yemen, and as far east as southern India, and these Jews spoke Greek and Aramaic and used the Septuagint.

The earliest Christian Bibles, all used the Septuagint, however, by the 4th century some Christian scholars were debating whether they should retranslate the Old Testament from the version the Jews were using, and some even suggested using the Samaritan version. Both suggestions were generally dismissed as heretical, as Jesus and the Apostles had quoted from the Septuagint, even though they had access to the Hebrew version then in use. This argument held in the West until the Middle Ages when Catholic Bibles switched to the Masoretic texts. In the east, Orthodox Bibles continued to use the Septuagint, as they do today. To the south, the Ethiopian Tewahedo Church continued to use the Septuagint, and across Asia, the Thomas Christians and Nestorians continued to use the Septuagint. Only in Western Europe were the later Masoretic texts adopted, abandoning the more ancient Septuagint, on the assumption that the Jews had copied their texts more faithfully than the Greeks had translated them. This assumption was carried forward into the Protestant Churches that broke off from the Catholic Church, and therefore almost all Protestant Bibles use the Masoretic texts for the basis of the Old Testament.

Unfortunately, this means that the earliest Christian writing is generally confusing and ignored by Protestants and Catholics. The earliest Christians of the first and second centuries quoted books that are no longer in the Bible, and as such, their writings are not always understood. Septuagint: Psalms and the Prayer of Manasseh is a 21st century translation aimed at correcting this problem.

One of the problems with academic translations of the Septuagint is the use of unfamiliar names or terms, as the Septuagint was written in Greek, and therefore many names are unrecognizable to modern English readers who are used to Hebrew-derived names. This project uses the more commonly understood Hebrew-derived names instead of their Greek translations, such as Canaan instead of Chanaan, and Melchizedek instead of Melchisedec. Common modern names are also used instead of either Greek or Hebrew terms when geographical locations are known, such as the archaeological name Uruk instead of the Greek Orech, or the Hebrew Erech, and the archaeological term Sumer instead of Shinar or Senar. While this could be argued as not being a correct academic procedure, it does fulfill the goal of making the translation easy to read and understand.

Psalms: Chapter 1

Blessed is the man who has not walked in the counsel of the impious, and has not stood in the way of sinners, and has not sat in the seat of pestilent men. His will is in the law of the Lord,[1] and on his law, he meditates day and night. He will be like a tree planted by the stream of waters, which will yield its fruit in its season, and its leaves will not fall off, and whatever he will do will prosper.

Not so the impious. Not so, but instead, like the chaff which the wind scatters away from the face of the earth. Therefore, the impious will not rise in judgment, nor sinners in the counsel of the just. The Lord knows the way of the righteous, but the way of the impious will perish.

Psalms: Chapter 1 Notes

1 Codex Vaticanus: cyriou (ΚΥΡΙΟΥ). Translation: lord
- Aleppo Codex: yhůh (יהוה)
- Leningrad Codex: yehovah (יְהֹוָה)
- Targum to Psalms: yeyā (??). Translation: Yah

This verse has not survived among the Dead Sea Scrolls, however, the term is found in some later verses.
- Dead Sea Scroll 1QPs^a: yhůh (𐤉𐤄𐤅𐤄), in chapter 86.
- Dead Sea Scroll 4QPs^a: yhůh (𐤉𐤄𐤅𐤄), in chapter 6.
- Dead Sea Scroll 4QPs^b: yhůh (𐤉𐤄𐤅𐤄), in chapter 92.

- Dead Sea Scroll 4QPs^c: yhůh (𐤉𐤄𐤅𐤄), in chapter 18.
- Dead Sea Scroll 4QPs^d: yhůh (𐤉𐤄𐤅𐤄), in chapter 147.
- Dead Sea Scroll 4QPs^e: yhůh (𐤉𐤄𐤅𐤄), in chapter 125.
- Dead Sea Scroll 4QPs^f: yhůh (𐤉𐤄𐤅𐤄), in chapter 107.
- Dead Sea Scroll 4QPs^g: yhůh (𐤉𐤄𐤅𐤄), in chapter 119.
- Dead Sea Scroll 4QPs^h: yhůh (𐤉𐤄𐤅𐤄), in chapter 119.
- Dead Sea Scroll 4QPs^k: yhůh (𐤉𐤄𐤅𐤄), in chapter 135.
- Dead Sea Scroll 4QPs^m: yhůh (𐤉𐤄𐤅𐤄), in chapter 87.
- Dead Sea Scroll 4QPs^o: yhůh (𐤉𐤄𐤅𐤄), in chapter 115.
- Dead Sea Scroll 4QPs^q: yhůh (𐤉𐤄𐤅𐤄), in chapter 31.
- Dead Sea Scroll 4QPs^r: yhůh (𐤉𐤄𐤅𐤄), in chapter 27.
- The Great Psalms Scroll: yhůh (𐤉𐤄𐤅𐤄), in chapter 102.
- Dead Sea Scroll 11QPs^c: yhůh (𐤉𐤄𐤅𐤄), in chapter 12.
- Dead Sea Scroll Nahal Hever Psalms: yhůh (𐤉𐤄𐤅𐤄), in chapter 12.
- Dead Sea Scroll MasPs^a: yhůh (𐤉𐤄𐤅𐤄), in chapter 81.

The name Yahweh (יהוה) was transliterated as Iaw (Ιαω) in some later books of the Septuagint, however, no early copies of Psalms survive that include the name Iaw. The name Yhůh (יהוה) is in almost all fragments of Psalms found among the Dead Sea Scrolls, however, all of these scrolls have been dated to the Hasmonean Dynasty or later, and most are in the Assyrian "block" script, the official script of the Hasmonean Dynasty. There are a few exceptions though, 11QPs^a is a fragment of Psalms written in Hebrew which includes the name Yhůh (𐤉𐤄𐤅𐤄) in the Canaanite script, however, dates to the Herodian Dynasty, a century after Simon the Zealot's Hebrew translation of the Aramaic texts that added the name

Iaw. As there is no evidence of Iaw being in Psalms before Simon's translation, the direct translation of Lord from κυρίου is used.

Psalms: Chapter 2

Why did the foreigners rage, and the nations imagine vain things? The kings of the earth stood up, and the rulers allied themselves together, against the Lord, and against his appointed,[1] saying, "Let us break through their bonds, and throw off their yoke from us."

He who lives in the sky[2] will laugh and ridicule them, and the Lord[3] will mock them. He will speak to them in anger then, and say to them with his fury, "I have been made king by him on Zion,[4] his holy mountain, and declare the ordinance of the Lord."

The Lord said to me, "You are my son, today I have adopted you. Ask me, and I will give you the foreigners for your inheritance, and to the edges of the earth as your possession. You will rule them with an iron mace, you will dash them in pieces like a potter's vessel."

Now, therefore, understand you kings, be instructed all you who judge the earth. Serve the Lord in fear, and rejoice in him with trembling. Accept correction if at any time the Lord is angry, and you should perish from the righteous way, whenever his anger will be suddenly started, blessed are all those who trust in him."

Psalms: Chapter 2 Notes

1 Codex Vaticanus: christou (ΧΡΙϹΤΟΥ). General translation: Christ (or savior)

• Aleppo Codex: mšyh (מָשִׁיח). Translation: messiah (or appointed)

• Leningrad Codex: moshch (מָשִׁיחַ). Translation: messiah (or appointed)

• Targum to Psalms: minṣê (מִנְצֵי). Translation: messiah (or appointed)

The term found in the Masoretic texts was used in Canaanite languages since at least the Late Bronze Age, where it appeared as mšh (𐎎𐎌𐎅) in both Ugaritic. The Aramaic word the Greeks translated was likely mšh (לۆשׂה), meaning anointed or savior, which was the meaning of christou (χριστου) in pre-Christian times.

2 Codex Vaticanus: ouranoes (ΟΥΡΑΝΟΙϹ). Translations: skies, that which is above the sky

• Aleppo Codex: šmym (שָׁמַיִם). Translations: sky (or universe, the sky, Shamayim)

• Leningrad Codex: shamayim (שָׁמַיִם). Translations: sky (or universe, the sky, Shamayim)

• Targum to Psalms: šemayā (שְׁמַיָא). Translation: sky (or skies)

While Shamayim (שָׁמַיִם) can refer to the sky god, in this verse it is clear that the vaulted sky is being referenced, which is further clarified later in Psalms when the sky above the sky is referred to.

3 Codex Vacticanus: o cyrios (Ο ΚΥΡΙΟC). Translation: the lord (or the master)

- Dead Sea Scroll 1QPs^a: -dny (נדי-), in chapter 86. The word is missing the first letter but is otherwise the Aramaic loan word found in the Masoretic texts.

- Dead Sea Scroll 4QPs^a: ådny (אדני), in chapter 38.

- Dead Sea Scroll 4QPs^e: -důny (דוני-), in chapter 89.

- Dead Sea Scroll 5QPs: ådůny (אדוני), in chapter 130.

- Dead Sea Scroll 11QPs^c: ådůny (אדוני). Translation: my lord.

- Aleppo Codex: ådny (אדני). Translation: my Lord

- Leningrad Codex: adonai (אֲדֹנָי). Translation: my lord

- Targum to Psalms: yyā ('‍'). Translation: Yah

The Leningrad Codex and Aleppo Codex use the Aramaic spelling of ådny (אדני), while some of the Dead Sea Scrolls use the Hebrew spelling, and others use the Aramaic. This confirms that the Hebrew translation was made directly from the Aramaic, and not from Greek or Canaanite, and also shows the Hebrew translations were still being finalized under the Herodian Dynasty.

The fact that the translators at the Library of Alexandria translated both the terms that ended up being Yhůh (יהוה) and ådny (אדני) in the Leningrad Codex and Aleppo Codex as Lord (Κύριοσ), suggests the Aramaic text they were working from used two terms, both meaning Lord. The two Aramaic words that translate as "lord" were ådny (אדני) and bôlå (בעלא). As the Hebrew texts are using a Hebrew transliteration of ådny, it suggests the term the Hasmoneans

23

replaced with Yhǔh, was bôlå (ℵ𝐿ᵛ𐤉), which is Ba'al (בַּעַל) in Hebrew.

4 Codex Vacticanus: Siôn (ⲥⲓⲱⲛ)

- Dead Sea Scroll 4QPs^b: ṣyǔn (צᵕᵕֿן), in chapter 102
- Dead Sea Scroll 5QPs: ṣyǔn (צᵕᵕֿן), in chapter 125
- Aleppo Codex: ṣyǔn (צᵕᵕֿן)
- Leningrad Codex: tziyyon (צִיּוֹן)
- Targum to Psalms: the name is missing from the verse

This name is generally transliterated into English as Zion. The Hebrew term is composed of the words ṣy (צי), meaning "fleet" in Hebrew, and the name ôn (ן‎ֹ). Ôn (Ων) was the name of Moses' God in the Septuagint, and the god of the Temple of Ôn in Samaria in the Book of Hosea, which was spelled as aven (אָוֶן) in the Leningrad Codex. The Hebrew word ṣy was derived from the Phoenician word ṣy (𐤑𐤉), meaning "ship," itself derived from the Egyptian word djåy (𓊪𓏭𓏲𓏏), meaning "barge." The term appears to have been adopted by the Canaanites by the Middle Kingdom era of Egyptian history, as the city of Sydǔn (𐤑𐤉𐤃𐤍), incorporated the word, as part of the city's name, which translates as "Ship Lord," because the Middle Kingdom era built most of their long range trading vessels in the region.

As the Akkadian cuneiform word Ān (𒀭) translates as "sky," "star," and "god," it suggests that the Canaanite name Zion, referred to the Solar Barge. The spelling of Jerusalem shifted from "evening land" to "city of peace," over time. The name was spelled as Úru Šalim^{ki} (𒌷𒊮𒆠) in Old

Akkadian, meaning either "light of Shalim land" or "setting sun land," depending on how the term is translated. Shalim (𐤔𐤋𐤌) was the Canaanite god of evening, married to the virgin goddess Asherah, and father of the lunar deity Adoni.

During the Old Akkadian Empire, the region around Jerusalem was in the borderlands of the Akkadian and Egyptian civilizations, suggesting the Akkadians viewed it as the most western land before the end of their empire. During the subsequent Neo-Sumerian era the name was ᵘʳᵘÚrušalim (𒌷𒊩𒆷𒁽𒌝), meaning "city of Shalim," indicating that there was a city there. The Egyptian execration texts from the era also spelled the name of the city as Úrŭšalim (𓂋�𓏤) in the Hieratic script, confirming that it was a commonly known name by the Middle Kingdom.

In the subsequent Old Babylonian language, the name was ᵘʳᵘÚrušalimᵏⁱ (𒌷𒊩𒆷𒁽𒌝𒆠), meaning "city of light of Shalim land," or "city of sunset land." In Neo-Assyrian the city was known as ᵘʳᵘUrsaliimma (𒌷�), meaning "city of peace" while in Neo-Babylonian it was known as ᵘʳᵘUrsaliimma (𒌷), also meaning "city of peace." Shalim was the Canaanite version of Atum, the god of the evening, and one of the solar gods of Egypt. As the solar gods were seen as healing gods by the Egyptians, this explains why the "blind and the lame" were in Zion.

Psalms: Chapter 3

A psalm of David, when he fled from the presence of his son Absalom.

Lord,[1] why are those who afflict me multiplied? Many rise up against me. Many say concerning my mind,[2] "There is no deliverance for him by his God."

Separate the psalm.[3]

But you, Lord, are my helper, my glory, and the one that lifts up my head. I cried to the Lord with my voice, and he heard me out of his holy mountain.

Separate the psalm.

I lay down and slept and I awoke, for the Lord will help me. I will not be afraid of the tens of thousands of people who are surrounding me. Rise, Lord, deliver me, my god, for you have struck all who were my enemies without cause and you have broken the teeth of sinners. Deliverance is the Lord's and your blessing is on your people.

Psalms: Chapter 3 Notes

1 Codex Vacticanus: cyrie (ⲕⲩⲣⲓⲉ). Translation: sir (or lord)
- Aleppo Codex: yhŭh (יהוה)
- Leningrad Codex: yehvah (יְהוָֹה)
- Targum to Psalms: yeyā (?). Translation: Yah

The Greek translation uses the term cyrie (κύριε), meaning, "sir," or "lord," as a proper name, indicating the Aramaic text used the term bôlå (ℵℓℽℷ), which was a title meaning "lord" in Aramaic and Canaanite. While the name Ba'al was generally applied to Ba'al Hadad in northern Canaan, it appears to have been primarily used to refer to the sun god Shamash in southern Canaan until the Babylonian at least conquest.

The Masoretic texts use the name Yehvah (יְהוָה) where the Septuagint used cyrie (κύριε), however, the Dead Sea Scrolls contain a number of variations, including Yhůh (יהוה) in Hebrew script, Yhůh (𐤉𐤄𐤅𐤄) in the Canaanite script, ådůny (אדוני) meaning "my lord," and Dead Sea Scroll 4QPsᵏ, which contains the damaged word ldů- (-לד), which is accepted as having been ldůd (לדוד), meaning "to David."

The Greeks did translate Yahweh from the Aramaic Yhů (𐤉𐤄𐤅) as Iaw (Ιαω) in some of the books of the Septuagint, however, there is no evidence of Iaw being in Psalms before Simon's Hebrew translation, the direct translation of Lord from cyrie (κύριε) is used.

2 Codex Vaticanus: psychê (ΨΥΧΗ). Translation: mind (or psyche, personality)
- Aleppo Codex: npšy (נפשי). Translation: spirit (or breath)
- Leningrad Codex: nafshi (נַפְשִׁי). Translation: spirit (or breath)
- Targum to Psalms: napšî (נַפְשִׁי). Translation: spirit (or breath)

Variations of "napshy" originally meant "breath" or "life," in Semitic languages, however, became "psyche" or "personality" in the Classical Era, and "soul" in the Medieval Era. In Akkadian napištu (𒐊) meant "life" and napašu (𒐊) meant "the breathe," while in the earlier Sumerian language, zi (𒐊) meant both "life" and "breath." In Ugaritic npš (𒐊) meant "breath," while in Imperial Aramaic npšå (ﬡﬢﬣ) meant "life." In Classical Aramaic and Hebrew the term took on the Greek meaning of "psyche" as well. In the Aramaic source text the Greeks translated, the word likely meant "life," however, this translation follows the Greek, and so "mind" is used.

3 Codex Vaticanus: diapsalma (ⲇⲓⲁⲯⲁⲗⲙⲁ): Translation: "separate the psalm"

• Aleppo Codex: slh (סלה). Translation: "to hang"

• Leningrad Codex: slh (סלה). Translation: "to hang"

• Targum to Psalms: the term was dropped from the Aramaic Targums

This term is generally used for a musical interlude, suggesting the original psalms were accompanied by music.

Psalms: Chapter 4

For the end, a Song of David among the Psalms.

When I called, my god Sydyk[1] heard me. "You have made room for me in tribulation. Pity me, and listen to my prayer. You sons of Adam, how long will you be heavy of heart? Do you, therefore, love vanity, and seek falsehood?"

Separate the psalm.

But know that the Lord has done wondrous things for his holy one, the Lord will hear me when I call to him. Be angry, but don't sin. Feel compunction in your beds for what you say in your hearts.

Separate the psalm.

Offer the sacrifices of Sydyk,[2] and trust in the Lord. Many say, "Who will show us good things? The light of your countenance, Lord, has been manifested towards us. You have put gladness into my heart, in the time of grain, grape juice, and olive oil,[3] when they were multiplied. I will lie down in peace and sleep, for you, Lord, have made me live securely.

Psalms: Chapter 4 Notes

1 Codex Vaticanus: o theos tês dicaeo mou (Ο ΘΕΟС ΤΗС ΔΙΚΑΙΟСΥΝΗСΜΟΥ). Translation: the god the law of mine

PSALMS: CHAPTER 4

- Aleppo Codex: ålhy ṣdqy (אלהי צדקי). Translation: god my justice (or god real-justice, my god Sydyk)
- Leningrad Codex: elohei tzidki (אֱלֹהֵי צִדְקִי). Translation: god my justice (or god real-justice, my god Sydyk)
- Targum to Psalms: ĕlôah ṣidqôtî (אֱלוֹהַ צִדְקוֹתִי). Translation: god of righteousness

This chapter has not survived among the Dead Sea Scrolls, and no other example of the term is found in Psalms, however, there are several references to Sydyk in Psalms that do support this as a reference to the god of justice, and not the concept of justice, such as the request for the Lord to listen to Sydyk in chapter 17, and the reference to the "gates of Sydyk" in chapter 118. In chapter 128, the term Lord Righteous (Κυριος Δικαιοσ) is used, mirrored by Yehvah Sydyk (יהוה צדיק) in the Masoretic text, but Lord Sydyk (אדני צדיק) in The Great Psalms Scroll from the Herodian dynasty, indicating that Yehvah did replace Sydyk in at least some if the Psalms.

Sydyk is a well-attested Canaanite god of Justice. His name was recorded in the Late Bronze Age as Ṣdq (𐎕𐎄𐎖) in Ugarit, and later in the Iron Age as Ṣdq (𐤑𐤃𐤒) in Canaanite and Ṣdq (𐡑𐡃𐡒) in Aramaic. The Phoenician Historian Philo of Byblos, who lived in the early 1st century AD, translated the name Sydyk as Dicaeon (Δίκαιον) in his translation of Sanchuniathon's writing from the Late Bronze Age, which is the same term used in the Septuagint. While ṣdq (צדק) does not refer to the god of Justice in Hebrew, it is used as the name of the planet Jupiter, which was named after Sydyk in

Aramaic and Canaanite, meaning that Sydyk was also once the god of Justice in Hebrew.

In the 1st century BC, the Judahite historian Philo of Alexandria claimed there were still worshipers of Sydyk (Συδυκ). In the 2nd century AD, Philo of Byblos collected the surviving works of Sanchuniathon from the late Bronze Age, which claimed that Sydyk and Misor were the sons of Amônos (Αμωνος) the Greek spelling of Ba'al Hmn (𐤋𐤏𐤁 𐤍𐤌𐤄), usually anglicized as Lord Hammon. Lord Hammon was the Canaanite equivalent of the North Egyptian Atum, South Egyptian Amen, and Kushite Aman. Like Amen, Hammon was viewed as a solar deity, a fertility god, and the king of the gods. He was also associated with infant sacrifice, suggesting he was the god "Moloch" (king) that was banned under the rule of Josiah, when Yahwism was adopted, suggesting some of the original Psalms were about Hammon. Hammon was also known by the title Ba'al Qarnim (𐤋𐤏𐤁 𐤒𐤓𐤍𐤌), meaning "Lord Horns" or "Lord Radiance" which mirrors the description found in the Psalms.

2 Codex Vaticanus: thysian dicaeosynês (ΘΥϹΊΑΝ ΔΙΚΑΙΟϹΎΝΗϹ). Translation: sacrifices of justice

• Aleppo Codex: zbhy-sdq (זבחי-צדק). Translation: sacrifices of justice (or Sydyk, planet Jupiter)

• Leningrad Codex: zivchei-tzedek (זִבְחֵי־צֶדֶק). Translation: sacrifices of justice (or Sydyk, planet Jupiter)

• Targum to Psalms: keniksat sidqā (כְּנִכְסַת צִדְקָא). Translation: righteous congregation

Sydyk is a well-attested Canaanite god of Justice. His name was recorded in the Late Bronze Age as Ṣdq (𒅎𒇻𒄿) in Ugarit, and later in the Iron Age as Ṣdq (𐤑𐤃𐤒) in Canaanite, and Ṣdq (𐡑𐡃𐡒) in Aramaic. The Phoenician Historian Philo of Byblos, who lived in the early 1st century AD, translated the name Sydyk as Dicaeon (Δίκαιον) in his translation of Sanchuniathon's writing from the Late Bronze Age, which is the root of the term used here. While ṣdq (צדק) does not refer to the god of Justice in Hebrew, it is used as the name of the planet Jupiter, which was named after Sydyk in Aramaic and Canaanite, meaning that Sydyk was also once the god of Justice in Hebrew. In the 1st century BC, the Judahite historian Philo of Alexandria claimed there were still worshipers of Sydyk (Συδυκ).

3 Codex Vacticanus: sitou cae oenou cae elaeou (ϹΙΤΟΥΚΑὶ ΟΙΝΟΥΚΑὶἐλλΙΟΥ). Translation: grain and wine and oil

- Aleppo Codex: dgnm ůtyrůšm (דגנס ותירושם). Translation: grains and grape juice
- Leningrad Codex: deganam vetirovosham (דְּגָנָם וְתִירוֹשָׁם). Translation: grains and grape juice

The Greek and Hebrew translations show an intentional redaction took place between the time that the Greek and Hebrew translations were made. The same trio found in the Greek texts was found in the Book of Hosea, where they were listed as the spirits or gods Dagon, Tirath, and Yitzhar. Dagon was an ancient grain god worshiped by Canaanites since the Bronze Age as deityDagan (𒀭𒁕𒃷) in Akkadian and Mari, Dgn (𒁕𒄀𒉌) in Ugaritic, and Dgn (𐤃𐤂𐤍) in

Canaanite and Punic, and Dagon (דָּגוֹן) in Hebrew. Tirath (◄─ ═►─◄) was mentioned in the Ugaritic texts and is believed to have been the god of grapes. Yitzhar (יִצְהָר) is an unknown spirit or god mentioned by Hosea with Dagon and Tirath, who is theorized to be the Canaanite god of olive oil, which was one of Canaan's largest exports in the time of Hosea. The fact that the trio is mentioned in the Septuagint's Psalms, but not the Hebrew translations implies that the trio was still worshiped by some in Judah during the Greek era that led into the Hasmonean Dynasty, when the Hebrew translations were made. The Greeks translated the names literally, except for Tirath, which became wine instead of "grape juice." In Classical Hebrew tyrvosh (תירוש) was grape juice that was up to one year old, and only partially fermented.

While the Aramaic text that the Greeks translated was probably referring to the trio of gods, that cannot be proven from the surviving Greek or Hebrew translations, so the literal translation from Greek is used.

Psalms: Chapter 5

For the end, concerning she who inherits. A psalm of David.

Listen to my words, Lord, pay attention to my song. Listen to the voice of my supplication, my king,[1] and my god,[2] to you, Lord, I will pray. In the morning you will hear my voice. In the morning I will wait for you, and will look up. For you are not a god who desires iniquity, and the worker of iniquity will not live with you, nor will the transgressors continue in your sight, as you hate, Lord, all those who work iniquity. You will destroy all that speak lies, as the Lord abhors the bloody and deceitful man. But I will enter your house through the greatness of your mercy. I will worship in your fear. Toward your holy temple, lead me, Lord, in your righteousness because of my enemies, make my way plain before your face. For there is no truth in their mouth, their heart is vain, their throat is an open sepulcher, and they have used their tongues deceitfully.

Judge them, God,[3] because of their counsels. Drive them out because of the abundance of their impiousness, for they have provoked you, Lord. But, let all those who trust in you be happy in you, they will celebrate forever, and you will live among them, and all who love your name will rejoice in you. You, I will praise, just you Lord. You have surrounded us with a shield of favor.

Psalms: Chapter 5 Notes

1 Codex Vaticanus: o basileus mou (**O ΒΑϹΙΛΕΥϹ ΜΟΥ**). Translation: the king of mine

- Aleppo Codex: mlky (מלכי). Translation: my king
- Leningrad Codex: malki (מַלְכִּי). Translation: my king
- Targum to Psalms: malkî (מַלְכִּי). Translation: my king

The usage of "king" as a metaphor for "god" is well established in ancient Semitic languages, including the Akkadian malku (𒈗), Canaanite mlk (𐤌𐤋𐤊), Aramaic malkå (𐡌𐡋𐡊), Sabaean mlk (𐩣𐩡𐩫), Hebrew mlk (מלך), Syriac malkå (ܡܠܟܐ). The Beta Israelite and Beta Abram communities that settled in Kush and farther south in the Ethiopian Highlands during the Classical era, carried the name Mlk south with them, giving rise to the Ge'ez äämïlakï (አምላክ), which continues to be the word for "God" in Ethiopia today among Tewahedo Christians. The term was also transliterated in the Septuagint's Amos as Moloch (Μολοχ) when referring to the god of Amman. In the context of this verse, the word is being used as a title, and not a name, and is therefore translated as "King."

2 Codex Vacticanus: o theos mou (**O ΘΕΟϹ ΜΟΥ**). Translation: the god of mine

- Aleppo Codex: ålhy (אלהי). Translation: my god (or my judge, my officer)
- Leningrad Codex: ålohai (אֱלֹהָי). Translation: my god (or my judge, my officer)
- Targum to Psalms: ålāhî (אֱלָהִי). Translation: my god

The definition of the Hebrew word ålh (אלה) has been debated, however, had been used to denote prince or king in Semitic languages for thousands of years by the time the Hebrew translation was made, including the Akkadian ilum (✴), Ugaritic îl (𒀭), Canaanite ålm (𐤀𐤋𐤌), and Aramaic ålhå (𐡀𐡋𐡄𐡀), which the Greeks translated as "god."

3 Codex Vacticanus: o theos (Ο ΘΕΟϹ). Translation: the god (or God)

- Dead Sea Scroll 4QPsᵃ: ålh- (-אלׄהׄ). The text is damaged in the word, and only "elohe" meaning "god" survives, however, the text likely originally included the term Elohim.
- Aleppo Codex: ålhym (אלהים). Translation: gods (in Aramaic, or goddesses in Hebrew, god in Neo-Assyrian, highest in Old Akkadian)
- Leningrad Codex: elohim (אֱלֹהִים). Translation: gods (in Aramaic, or goddesses in Hebrew, god in Neo-Assyrian, highest in Old Akkadian)
- Targum to Psalms: ĕlāhā (אֱלָהָא). Translation: god

The word in the Masoretic texts is commonly translated as "God," but is a plural form of the Aramaic ålhå (𐡀𐡋𐡄𐡀),

meaning "gods," or a plural form of the Hebrew elah (אֵלָה) meaning "goddesses."

The terms âlhym (ᴙᴢᴈ𝈿), and âlhym (𝈿^𝈤𝈦𝈡), are also direct transcriptions of the Neo-Assyrian word elium (𐎹𐎹𐎹), which by the Iron Age meant "god," indicating that text had previously been written in cuneiform, and was translated into Aramaic or Phoenician during the iron age. During the bronze age, the word alium (𐎹𐎹𐎹) referred to a specific god, ^{deity}Ān (✳✳) the highest god, and father of the other gods. His Akkadian name was derived from the word elûm (𐎹𐎹), meaning "higher," as the term was intended to convey the meaning of "highest." He was believed to live in the polar region of the sky, where the modern constellation of Draco is located, making him the highest in the sky, around which all the gods (stars) circled.

The term el elyon (אֵל עֶלְיוֹן), meaning "highest god," was translated into Hebrew in Genesis Psalms: Chapter 14, where the Greeks translated it as theô tô hypsistô (θεω τω ὑψίστω), also meaning "highest god." El Elyon is known to have been a major god of the Canaanites, called âl ûâlyn (𝈿^𝈡𝈦 𝈡𝈦), meaning "God and Highest" in an Aramaic language Sefire Treaty from circa 750 BC. The Greek translations of Sanchuniathon's bronze age writing that has survived to the present, referred to the primordial creator god of the Canaanites as Elioun (Ελιουν), which appears to be the same god. According to Sanchuniathon, Elioun was the highest (ὑψιστος) god, who made the sky and the land, and they made the rest of the gods.

During the Old Babylonian and Old Assyrian eras, the gods Marduk and Ashur, the national gods of Babylon and Assyria, replaced the Akkadian An as the primary god of the Mesopotamian pantheons, and by the iron age, the word elium had came to mean "god," explaining why the Aramaic term ålhym (ﬡﬥﬢﬤﬣ) would have been interpreted as "god," by the Greeks.

Psalms: Chapter 6

For the end, among the Hymns, for the eighth. A psalm of David.

Lord, don't rebuke me in your anger nor punish me in your anger. Pity me, Lord, for I am weak. Heal me, Lord, for my bones are damaged. My mind also is grievously hurt, but you, Lord, how long? Return, Lord, save my mind. Save me for your mercy's sake, for in death no man remembers you, and who will praise you from Sheol?[1]

I am tired and groaning, I will wet my bed every night. I will water my couch with tears. My eye is troubled because of my anger, I am worn out because of all my enemies. Depart from me, all you who work iniquity, as the Lord has heard the voice of my weeping. The Lord has listened to my petition. The Lord has accepted my prayer. Let all my enemies be put to shame and greatly troubled. Let them be turned back and grievously put to shame quickly.

Psalms: Chapter 6 Notes

1 Codex Vaticanus: thanatô (ⲐⲀⲚⲀⲦⲱ). Translation: death
- Aleppo Codex: šåůl (שאול). Translation: Sheol
- Leningrad Codex: she'ovl (שְׁאוֹל). Translation: Sheol

• Targum to Psalms: šeôl (שְׁאוֹל). Translation: Sheol

Sheol was the dusty underworld of the ancient Israelite religion, which is also sometimes translated as "grave."

Psalms: Chapter 7

A psalm of David, which he sang to the Lord because of the words of Hushai the son of the southerner.[1]

Lord my god,[2] in you I have trusted, save me from all those who persecute me, and deliver me. In case at any time the enemy seizes my mind like a lion and there is none to ransom or to save. Lord my god, if I have done this, (if there is unrighteousness in my hands,) if I have repaid with evil those who repaid me with good, may I then die pointlessly through my enemies. Let the enemy persecute my mind, and take it, and let him trample my life to the ground, and lay my glory in the dust.

Separate the psalm.

Rise, Lord, in your anger. Be praised in the utmost boundaries of my enemies. Awake, Lord my god, according to the decree which you commanded. "The alliance of the nations will surround you, and for this cause do you return on high. Lord, judge the nations, judge me, Lord, according to my righteousness, and according to the innocence that is in me. Let the iniquity of sinners come to an end, and then you will direct the righteous, who search the hearts and minds, God.

Sydyk is my helper from the god who saves those upright in heart. God is a righteous judge, strong, and patient, not inflicting vengeance every day. If you will not repent, he will furbish his sword, he has bent his bow and made it ready. On it, he has fitted the instruments of death, and he has completed his arrows for the raging ones. Look, he has struggled with unrighteousness, he has conceived trouble and brought out iniquity. He has opened a pit and dug it up, and he will fall into the ditch which he has made. His trouble will return on his own head, and his unrighteousness will come down on his own crown. I will give thanks to the Lord according to his righteousness, and I will praise the name of Lord Elyon.[3]

Psalms: Chapter 7 Notes

1 Codex Vaticanus: Iemeni (ιεΜεΝι)

• Aleppo Codex: ymyny (יְמִינִי). Translations: right (direction), right-handed, southerner

• Leningrad Codex: yemini (יְמִינִי). Translation: right (direction), right-handed, southerner

• Targum to Psalms: šēbeṭ binyāmin (שֵׁבֶט בִּנְיָמִן). Translation: tribe of Benjamin

If this psalm was written by or for the Hushai in the Septuagint's 2nd Kingdoms (Masoretic Samuel), who was a close friend of David, that particular Hushai was referred to as being from a town called Archi, in the allotment of Ephraim, near Bethel (generally accepted as modern Beitin in the

Palestinian West Bank.) Based on the meaning of the Hebrew word, the translation of "southerner" is used.

2 Codex Vaticanus: cyrie o theos (ⲔⲨⲢⲒⲈⲞⲐⲈⲞⲤ).
Translation: lord the god
- Aleppo Codex: yhůh ålhy (יהוה אלהי). Translations: Yhůh my god
- Leningrad Codex: yehvah elohai (יְהוָ֣ה אֱלֹהַ֑י). Translation: Yahweh my god
- Targum to Psalms: yeyā ĕlōhay (יְ֝֗יָ אֱלֹהַ֑י). Translation: Yah my god

The Aramaic source texts that Greeks translated from would have read "Lord my god" (𐡍𐡕𐡋𐡍 𐡍𐡋𐡏𐡉), as the other Aramaic term meaning lord, ådny (𐡀𐡃𐡍𐡉), survives in the Hebrew translations of Psalms. Many gods were called Ba'al by their worshipers. In this verse, the Ba'al was clearly not Hadad, the northern Canaanite god of thunder, but appears to be the sun god Hammon, who was the dominant Ba'al worshiped in southern and central Canaan during the Egyptian New Kingdom era.

3 Codex Vaticanus: cyriou tou hypsistou (ⲔⲨⲢⲒⲞⲨⲦⲞⲨ Ⲩ︢ⲨⲒⲤⲦⲞⲨ). Translation: lord of highest
- Aleppo Codex: yhůh ôlyůn (יהוה עליון). Translations: Yhůh highest
- Leningrad Codex: yehvah elyovn (יְהוָ֣ה עֶלְי֑וֹן). Translation: Yehvah highest

47

• Targum to Psalms: ĕlāhā ilāâ (אֱלָהָא עִלָּאָה). Translation: god ascended

The Highest is a reference to God, or a god, found in many ancient religions in the region. According to the Torah, the ancient people of Jerusalem worshiped El Elyon, which translates as "Highest God" when Abram passed through the region.

Psalms: Chapter 8

For the end, concerning the wine presses, a psalm of David.

Lord our lord,[1] how wonderful is your name in all the earth! For your magnificence is praised above Shamayim. Out of the mouth of babes and infants you have perfected praise, because of your enemies, that you might put down the enemy and avenger. For I will consider the sky[2] the work of your fingers, and the moon[3] and star[4] which you have established. What is man, that you remember him? Or the son of Adam,[5] that you visit him? You made him a little less than messengers, and you have crowned him with glory and honor, and you have set him over the works of your hands. You have put all things under his feet, sheep and all cows, yes and the livestock of the field, the birds of the sky, and the fish of the sea, the creatures passing through the paths of the sea.

Lord our lord, how wonderful is your name on all the Earth!

Psalms: Chapter 8 Notes

1 Codex Vaticanus: cyrie o cyrios êmôn (ΚΥΡΙΕΟΚΥΡΙΟϹ ΗΜΩΝ). Translation: lord the lord of ours

- Aleppo Codex: yhǔh ǎdnynǔ (יהוה אדנינו). Translations: Yhǔh our lord
- Leningrad Codex: yehvah adoneinu (יְהֹוָה אֲדֹנֵינוּ). Translation: Yehvah our lord
- Targum to Psalms: yeyā ĕlāhā (יְיָ אֱלָהָא). Translation: Yah god

The Aramaic source texts that Greeks translated from would have read bôlǎ ǎdny (ᵃᵧᵀᴎ ᴎᴸᵘᴣ), as the other Aramaic term meaning lord, ǎdny (ᵃᵧᵀᴎ), survives in the Hebrew translation. Many gods were called Ba'al by their worshipers. In this verse, the Ba'al was clearly not Hadad, the northern Canaanite god of thunder, and appears to be the sun god Shamash, who was the dominant Ba'al worshiped in southern Canaan during the Egyptian New Kingdom era.

2 Codex Vaticanus: ouranous (ΟΥΡΑΝΟΥϹ). Translation: sky (or vaulted sky)
- Aleppo Codex: šmyk (שמיך). Translations: your sky (or your name)
- Leningrad Codex: shameicha (שָׁמֶיךָ). Translation: your sky (or your name)
- Targum to Psalms: šemāyik (שְׁמָיִךְ). Translation: your name

3 Codex Vaticanus: selênên (ϹΕΛΗΝΗΝ). Translation: moon (or Selene, month)

• Dead Sea Scroll Nahal Hever Psalms: -ḥ (**ח-**). Only the final letter of the word survives, however, it is enough to prove it was present in the texts.

• Aleppo Codex: yrḥ (**ירח**). Translations: moon (or Yarikh, month)

• Leningrad Codex: yareach (**יָרֵחַ**). Translation: moon (or Yarikh, month)

• Targum to Psalms: sîhărā (**סִיהֲרָא**). Translation: moon

As there was no difference between the moon and the god of the moon in the era the text was written, either translation could be used, however, the word moon makes more sense in a sentence with sky and stars than the name of the god.

4 Codex Vaticanus: asteras (**ΑϹΤΕΡΑϹ**). Translation: star

• Dead Sea Scroll Nahal Hever Psalms: kŭkb-m (**כוכב-ם**). One letter of the word survives, however, it is enough to prove the plural form was used in the texts.

• Aleppo Codex: kŭkbym (**כוכבים**). Translations: stars

• Leningrad Codex: chovchavim (**כּוֹכְבִים**). Translation: stars

• Targum to Psalms: kōkebayā (**כֹכְבַיָא**). Likely a scribal error of kŭkbå (**ΚϪϪΕϜ**), suggesting the scribe's primary language was Punic, as the Punic spelling kkb (**ϞⲮⲮ**). If so, the Aramaic Targum is much older than generally recognized.

The fact that the Greeks translated the singular form of the word, "star" instead of "stars," implies the Aramaic text the Greeks translated used the singular form kŭkbå (**ΑϧⲮΚϪ**). Both the Semitic and Greek languages had used singular and plural forms for "star" and "stars" for more than a thousand years by the time the Library of Alexandria translated the text, making it unlikely the Greeks mistranslated the term. This implies a specific star was intended, likely Venus. As the sun is not mentioned in this psalm, it seems likely that the lord implied was the sun-god Shalim, and the psalm was originally dedicated to the Jerusalem trinity of the sun, Venus, and moon. At Baalbek, in Lebanon, the trinity was known as Ba'al, Astarte, and Adonis. During the Roman era, the Canaanite gods became associated with Jupiter, Venus, and Mercury, as the Romans considered Jupiter the supreme god, and Mercury the messenger god, however, the Canaanite version of the trinity was based on the trinity worshiped at Iůnů (Heliopolis, Aven), in Egypt, composed of Atum (☒), Hathor (☒☒), while his son was known as Iôhů (☒☒☒☒) in the Second Intermediate Period and the subsequent New Kingdom, when Egypt ruled Canaan. Both the city of Iůnů and a temple of Atum (Per-Atum), are mentioned as places in Egypt associated with the Israelite patriarchs Joseph, Moses, and Aaron, supporting the connection between the trinities of Jerusalem and Heliopolis.

5 Codex Vacticanus: huios anthrôpou (ΥΙΟϹΑΝΘΡѠΠΟΥ). Translation: son of a human

• Aleppo Codex: bn-ådm (בֶּן-אָדָם). Translations: son of man (or decedents of Adam, human)

• Leningrad Codex: ven-adam (בֶן־אָדָם). Translation: son of man (or decedents of Adam, human)

• Targum to Psalms: bar nāšā (בַר נָשָׁא). Translation: son of uplifted

The term "ben-ādām" is used throughout the Masoretic Texts, and translated into Greek as "huios anthrôpou" in the Septuagint, meaning "son of human," however, while this is consistent with the meaning in the Classical Era, it does not appear to have been the original meaning. Adam is accepted as meaning "man" in many Semitic languages, including the Semitic Ugaritic ådm (𐎀𐎄𐎎), Canaanite ådm (𐤀𐤃𐤌), Aramaic ådm (𐡀𐡃𐡌), Hebrew ådm (אָדָם), Syriac ådam (ܐܕܡ), Arabic ådam (آدم), and Ge'ez äädami (አዳም). The term does not universally mean "man" in Semitic languages, it can also mean "subject," as in the Sabaean ådm (𐩱𐩵𐩣), or "slave," as in the Ge'ez domi (ዶም). The oldest forms of the name in Akkadian Cuneiform suggest it may have been the original Semitic name of Canaan/Phoenicia.

The Akkadian words that share the common root of adm include adaammu (𒀉𒁕𒄠𒈬) meaning "blood," adamatum (𒀉𒁕𒈠𒌈) meaning dye, and adamu (𒀉𒁕𒈬) meaning "red cloth" or "noble." The two names for Canaan/Phoenicia are derived from similar terms used by the two foreign nations that generally ruled the region. The name Canaan is accepted as being derived from the name Akkadian name ᵏᵘʳKinaaḫna (𒆠𒈾𒀪𒈾), found in the Amarna Letters, and meaning "Land of Kinaḫḫu," in Akkadian. Kinaḫḫu is itself believed to mean "red" or "purple" in the indigenous Hurrian languages. Likewise, the Greek name Phoenician (φοῖνιξ), is accepted as being derived from the Mycenaean Linear-B ponikijo (𐀡𐀛𐀑𐀍) meaning "crimson." Both names appear to have been used by the Canaanites/Phoenicians in the early Iron-Age, as Knôn (𐤊𐤍𐤍) and Pnym (𐤐𐤍𐤉𐤌). The term ådm

(𐤀𐤃𐤌) continued to be used as the regional name for southern Canaan in the early Iron Age, as the region of Edom, however, the usage in the Ugaritic Texts and Masoretic Texts suggests it was once the Semitic name for Canaan. The change in the meaning of the word, from noble in Mesopotamia to person in Canaan, to subject in Arabia, and slave in Ethiopia, suggests these people were indigenous to Canaan, and for some time ruled Mesopotamia in the Akkadian era. The translation of "son of Adam" is used in this translation.

Psalms: Chapter 9

For the end, concerning the secrets of the son. A psalm of David.

I will give thanks to you, Lord, with my whole heart, I will recount all your wonderful works. I will be glad and praise you, I will sing your name to the Highest. When my enemies are turned back, they will be feeble and perish in your presence. For you have maintained my cause and my right, you sat on the throne that judges righteousness. You have rebuked the nations, and the impious one has perished, you have blotted out their name forever, even forever and ever.

The swords of the enemy have failed, and you have destroyed cities. Their memory has been destroyed through noise, but the Lord endures forever. He has prepared his throne for judgment. He will judge the world in righteousness, he will judge the nations in uprightness. The Lord also has become a refuge for the poor, a seasonable help, in affliction. Let those who know your name hope in you, for you, Lord, have not failed those who diligently seek you.

Sing praises to the Lord, who lives on Zion. Declare his dealings among the nations. For he remembered them, in making inquisition for blood, he has not forgotten the supplication of the poor. Have mercy on me, the Lord. Look on my affliction which I allow of my enemies, you that lift me from the gates of death, that I may declare all your praises in the gates of the daughter of Zion. I will celebrate your salvation. The nations are caught in the destruction that they planned. In the very snare which they hid is their foot taken. The Lord is known for executing judgments, the sinner is taken in the works of his hands.

A song of consideration.

Let sinners be driven away into Sheol and also all the nations that forget God. For the poor will not be forgotten forever, the patience of the needy ones will not perish forever. Rise, Lord, don't let man prevail. Let the nations be judged before you. Appoint, Lord, a lawgiver over them, and let the nations know that they are men.

Separate the psalm.

Why do you stand far off, Lord? Why do you overlook us in times of need and affliction? While the impious one behaves proudly, the poor are inflamed, and the wicked are taken in the cunning counsels which they imagine. Because the sinner praises himself for the desires of his heart, and the unjust one blesses himself. The sinner has provoked the Lord, according to the abundance of his anger, he will not seek after him. God is not before him. His ways are profane at all times, and your judgments are removed from before him. He will gain mastery over all his enemies. For he has said in his heart," I will not be moved, continuing without evil from generation to generation, whose mouth is full of cursing, and bitterness, and fraud, under his tongue are trouble and pain."

He lies in wait with rich men in secret places, to kill the innocent. His eyes look against the poor. He lies in wait in secret as a lion in his den. He lies in wait to ravish the poor, to ravish the poor when he draws him after him. He will bring him down in his snare. He will bow down and fall when he has mastered the poor. For he has said in his heart, "God has forgotten. He has turned away his face so as never to look."

Rise, Lord God! Let your hand be lifted, don't forget the poor. Why have the wicked provoked God? For he has said in his heart, "He will not require it." You see it, for you do observe trouble and anger, to deliver them into your hands. The poor have been left to you. You were a helper to the orphan.

Break the arm of the sinner and wicked man. His sin will be searched for, but will not be found. The Lord will reign forever, even forever and ever. The nations will perish out of his land. The Lord has heard the desire of the poor. Your ear has inclined to the preparation of their heart, to plead for the orphan and afflicted, that man may no longer brag on the earth.

Psalms: Chapter 10

A psalm of David.

In the Lord I have put my trust, how will you say to my mind, "Flee to the mountains like a sparrow?" For look, the sinners have bent their bow, they have prepared their arrows for the quiver, to shoot under a dark moon for the upright in heart. For they have pulled down what you framed, but what has the righteous done?

The Lord is in his holy temple. The Lord's throne is in the skies. His eyes see the poor, his eyelids test the sons of Adam. The Lord tries the righteous and the impious, and he who loves unrighteousness hates his own mind. He will rain on sinners' snares, fire, and brimstone, and a stormy blast will be the portion of their cup. The Lord is righteous and loves righteousness, and he sees uprightness.

Psalms: Chapter 11

On the eighth. A psalm of David.

Save me, Lord, as the pious man has failed, and truth has become rare among the children of men. Everyone has spoken vanity to his neighbor, their lips are deceitful, and they have spoken with a double heart. Let the Lord destroy all the deceitful lips and the tongue that speaks great words who have said, "We will magnify our tongue. Our lips are our own, who is lord of us? Because of the misery of the poor, and because of the sighing of the needy now, I will arise," says the Lord. "I will set them in safety. I will speak to them openly."

The oracles of the Lord are pure oracles, as silver smelted in fire, proved a furnace of earth, purified seven times. You, Lord, will keep us and will preserve us, from this generation, and forever. The impious walk around, according to your greatness you have greatly praised the sons of Adam.

Psalms: Chapter 12

A psalm of David.

How long, Lord, will you forget me? Forever? How long will you turn away your face from me? How long will I take counsel in my mind, having sorrows in my heart daily? How long will my enemy be elevated over me? See me, hear me, Lord, my god, lighten my eyes, in case I sleep in death, in case at any time my enemy says, "I have defeated him!" My persecutors will celebrate if ever I should be moved. But I have trusted in your mercy. My heart will celebrate your salvation. I will sing to the Lord who has dealt bountifully with me, and I will sing psalms to the name of the Highest lord.

Psalms: Chapter 13

A psalm of David.

The fool has said in his heart, "There is no God."

They have corrupted themselves, and become abominable in their plans. None does anything good. There is not even one. The Lord looked down from the sky on the sons of Adam, to see if there were any that understood or searched for God. They have all left the way. They have united and become good for nothing. None does any good. Not even one. Their throat is an open sepulcher, and with their tongues, they have used deceit. The poison of asps is under their lips, whose mouth is full of cursing and bitterness. Their feet are swift to shed blood, and destruction and misery are their ways. The way of peace they have not known, and there is no fear of God in their eyes.

Will not all the workers of iniquity know, who eat up my people as they would eat bread? They have not called on the Lord. There they were alarmed with fear, whereas there is no fear when God is in the righteous generation. You have shamed the counsel of the poor because the Lord is his hope. Who will bring the salvation of Israel out of Zion? When the Lord brings back the captivity of his people, let Jacob rejoice, and Israel be glad.

Psalms: Chapter 14

A psalm of David.

Lord, who will stay in your tabernacle? Who will live on your holy mountain? He who walks blameless, and works righteousness, who speaks truth in his heart? He who has not spoken craftily with his tongue, nor has done evil to his neighbor or insulted those who lived nearest to him. In his sight, an evil worker is set at nothing, but he honors those who fear the Lord. He swears to his neighbor and does not disappoint him. He has not given his money on interest and has not received bribes against the innocent. He who does these things will never be moved.

Psalms: Chapter 15

A writing of David.

Protect me, Lord, for I have trusted in you. I said to the Lord, "You are my lord. For you do not need my good deeds."

On behalf of the sacred ones[1] who are in his land, he has praised all his pleasure in them. Their weaknesses have been multiplied, and afterward, they rushed. I will by no means assemble their bloody meetings, neither will I make mention of their names with my lips. The Lord is the portion of my inheritance and my cup. You are he that restores my inheritance to me. The lines have fallen to me in the best places, yes, I have a most excellent heritage. I will bless the Lord who has instructed me, and my reins too have punished me even during the night. I foresaw the Lord always before my face, for he is on my right hand, that I should not be moved. Therefore my heart rejoiced and my tongue celebrated, and also my flesh will rest in hope, because you will not leave my mind in Sheol, nor will you allow your holy one to see corruption. You have made known to me the ways of life, and you will fill me with joy with your countenance. At your right hand, there are delights forever.

Psalms: Chapter 15 Notes

1 Codex Vacticanus: agíois (ΑΓΙΟΙC). Translations: saints

• Aleppo Codex: qdůšym (קדושים). Translations: holy ones

• Leningrad Codex: kedoshim (קְדוֹשִׁים). Translation: holy ones

• Targum to Psalms: qadîšayā (קַדִּישַׁיָּא). Translation: holy one

The term qadeshim is the plural form of qadesh (קדוש), meaning "sacred."

Psalms: Chapter 16

A prayer of David.

Listen, Lord to my righteous prayer, and pay attention to my petition. Give ear to my prayer not spoken with deceitful lips.

Let my judgment come out from your presence. Let my eyes see righteousness. You have tested my heart, and you have visited me by night. You have tested me as with fire, and unrighteousness has not been found in me. I have decided that my mouth will not speak incorrectly.

As for the works of men, by the words of your lips, I have followed difficult paths. Direct my steps in your paths, so my steps don't slip. I have cried, for you heard me, "God, Incline your ear to me, and listen to my words. Show the marvels of your mercies, you that save those who hope in you. Keep me as the apple of your eye from those who resist your right hand. You will screen me by the covering of your wings, from the face of the impious that have afflicted me. My enemies have surrounded my mind. They have surrounded themselves with their own fat. Their mouth has spoken pride. They have now thrown me out and surrounded me. They have set their eyes to bow down to the ground. They laid wait for me like a lion ready for prey, and like a lion's whelp living in secret places."

Rise, Lord, prevent them and throw them down. Deliver my mind from the impious. Draw your sword, because of the enemies of your hand. Lord, destroy them from the earth! Scatter them in their life! Though their belly has been filled with your hidden treasures, they have been satisfied with uncleanness, and have left the remnant of their possessions to their babes. But I will appear in righteousness before your face. I will be satisfied when your glory appears.

Psalms: Chapter 17

A psalm of David, the servant of the Lord, the words which he spoke to the Lord, including the words of this song, on the day in which the Lord delivered him out of the hand of all his enemies, and the hand of Saul.

He said, "I will love you, Lord, my strength. The Lord is my firm support, and my refuge, and my deliverer, my god is my helper, I will trust in him. He is my defender, and the horn of my salvation, and my helper."

I will call on the Lord with praises, and I will be saved from my enemies. The pangs of Mot surrounded me, and the torrents of impiousness troubled me exceedingly. The pangs of Sheol came around me, the snares of Mot prevented me. When I was afflicted I called on the Lord and cried to my god. He heard my voice out of this holy temple, and my cry would enter before him, even into his ears. Then the earth shook and quaked, and the foundations of the mountains were disturbed and were shaken because God was angry with them. There went up a smoke in his anger, and fire burst into a flame at his presence. Coals were started in it.

He lowered the sky and came down, and thick darkness was under his feet. He mounted the sphinx[1] and flew, and he flew on the wings of winds. He made darkness his secret place, and around him was his tabernacle, even dark water in the clouds of the air. At the brightness before him the clouds passed with hail and coals of fire. The Lord also thundered from the sky, and the Highest spoke his voice.

He sent out his weapons to scatter them with a great deal of lightning and routed them. The springs of waters appeared, and the foundations of the world were exposed, at your rebuke, Lord, at the blasting of the breath of your anger. He sent from on high and took me, he drew me to himself in the upper waters. He will deliver me from my mighty enemies, and from those who hate me, for they are stronger than I. They prevented me in the day of my affliction, but the Lord was my defense against them.

He brought me out into a wide place, and he will deliver me because he has pleasure in me. The Lord will repay me according to my righteousness, and even according to the purity of my hands will he repay me. For I have kept the way of the Lord and have not wickedly departed from my God.

For all his judgments were before me, and his ordinances did not leave me. I will be blameless with him and will keep myself from my iniquity. The Lord will repay me according to my righteousness, and according to the purity of my hands before his eyes. With the holy, you will be holy, and with the innocent man, you will be innocent. With the excellent man, you will be excellent, and with the perverse, you will show perversion. For you will save the lowly people and will humiliate the eyes of the proud.

For you, Lord will light my lamp, my god, you will lighten my darkness. For by you will I be delivered from a troop, and by my god I will pass over a wall. As for my god, his way is perfect. The oracles of the Lord are tried in the fire. He is a protector of all those who trust in him.

For who is God but the Lord? And who is a god except for our god? It is God that girds me with strength and has made my way blameless, who strengthens my feet as deer's feet and sets me in high places. He instructs my hands for war, and you have made my arms like a bronze bow. You have made me the protection of my salvation, and your right hand has helped me, and your correction has upheld me to the end, yes, your correction itself will instruct me.

You have made room for my goings under me, and by footsteps did not fail. I will chase my enemies and overtake them, and I will not turn back until they are consumed. I will dash them to pieces and they will not be able to stand. They will fall under my feet.

For you have girded me with strength for war, you have beaten down under me all that rose against me. You have made my enemies turn their backs before me, and you have destroyed those who hated me. They cried, but there was no deliverer, even to the Lord, but he did not listen to them. I will grind them like the mud of the streets, and I will beat them small as the dust before the wind.

Deliver me from the insults of the people. Make me the ruler of the nations, peoples who I did not know served me, at the hearing of the ear they obeyed me. The strange children lied to me. The strange children grew old and fell away from their paths through lameness.

The Lord lives! Blessed be my god, and let the god of my salvation be praised. It is God who avenges me and has subdued the nations under me, my deliverer from angry enemies. You will set me on high above those who rise up against me. You will deliver me from the unrighteous man.

Therefore I will confess to you, Lord, among the nations, and sing to your name. God magnifies the deliverance of his king and deals mercifully with David his anointed, and his descendants, forever.

Psalms: Chapter 17 Notes

1 Codex Vacticanus: cheroubin (ⲭⲉⲣⲟⲩⲃⲓⲛ)

• Codex Sinaiticus: cheroub (ⲭⲉⲣⲟⲩⲃ)

• Septuagint manuscript 55: cheroubim (χόβουμμ)

• Aleppo Codex: krûb (כרוב). Translations: cherub (or griffin, sphinx)

• Leningrad Codex: keruv (כְּרוּב). Translation: cherub (or griffin, sphinx)

• Bohairic manuscripts: kheroubim (ⲭⲉⲣⲟⲩⲃⲓⲙ)

• Targum to Psalms: kerûbîn (כְּרוּבִין). Translation: cherubs

The Codex Vaticanus term is a transliteration of the Aramaic word krûbyn (𐡊𐡓𐡅𐡁𐡉𐡍), the plural form of the word krûb (כרוב), found in the Hebrew texts, and the Codex Sinaiticus. The transliteration of cheroubim (χερουβιμ) found in some later Greek translations is likely copied from the Coptic kheroubim (ⲭⲉⲣⲟⲩⲃⲓⲙ), itself based on the Hebrew krûbym (כרובים), although not Hebrew versions of the verse survive that include the plural form of the word. As the Sinaiticus and Vaticanus codices are equally old, and the Hebrew texts support the Sinaiticus reading, the singular form is used there.

The word "cherub" (𐤊𐤓𐤅𐤁 / כרוב / 𐡊𐡓𐡅𐡁 / 𓐍𓂋𓃀) was the West Semitic term for the mythical creature generally called a "griffin" today. Based on the archaeological record of Canaan, it appears that the concept of the cherub was based on the Egyptian sphinx, as the earliest cherub statues found in Canaan were Egyptian statues of sphinxes. Archaeologists are not sure if the griffins of Anatolia were based on the

Canaanite cherub, or the Egyptian sphinxes directly, however, all three mythical beings are closely related in the archaeological record. At the time of David, the Israelite statues were still shaped like sphinxes, so that word is used here.

In Egyptian religion, the sun god Horus rose into the sky each morning on the back of the sphinx, supporting the reading of the early psalms being about a solar deity, such as Shalim, the god David named his son Solomon after.

Psalms: Chapter 18

A psalm of David.

Shamayim declares the glory of God, the creation of his hands is shown in the framework[1] day to day,[2] speaking words night to night[3] to proclaim knowledge. There are no speeches or words, in which their voices are not heard. Their voice has gone out to all the earth, and their words to the ends of the world.

In the sun he is accustomed to living, and he comes out like a bridegroom out of his chamber. He will celebrate like Orion[4] running his course. His going out is from the extremity of the sky, and his circuit to the other end of the sky, and no one will be hidden from his heat.

The law of the Lord is perfect, converting minds, the testimony of the Lord is faithful, instructing babes. The ordinances of the Lord are right, rejoicing the heart, the commandment of the Lord is bright, enlightening the eyes. The fear of the Lord is pure, enduring forever and ever, the judgments of the Lord are true and justified altogether. To be desired more than gold, and very precious stones, sweeter also than honey and the honeycomb. For your servant follows them, in following them there is great reward. Who will understand his transgressions? Purge my sins from me. Spare your servant the attack of strangers, if they do not gain dominion over me, then I will be blameless, and I will be clear from great sin.

So will the sayings of my mouth, and the meditation of my heart, be pleasing continually before you, Lord, my helper, and my redeemer.

Psalms: Chapter 18 Notes

1 Codex Vacticanus: stereôma (ϹΤΕΡΕѠΜΑ). Translations: framework (or foundation, firmament, ceiling)

• Aleppo Codex: rqyô (רְקִיעַ). Translations: a concave vaulted sky above the flat earth

• Leningrad Codex: rakia' (רָקִיעַ). Translation: a concave vaulted sky above the flat earth

• Targum to Psalms: awîrā (אֲוִירָא). Translation: air (or atmosphere)

2 Codex Vacticanus: êmera tê êmera (ΗΜΕΡΑΤΗΗΜΕΡΑ). Translation: day (or Hemera) the (or she) day

• Aleppo Codex: yǔm lyǔm (יוֹם לְיוֹם). Translations: day to day

• Leningrad Codex: yovm leyovm (יוֹם לְיוֹם). Translation: day to day

• Targum to Psalms: yômā leyômā (יוֹמָא לְיוֹמָא). Translation: day to day

The Greek translation is referencing Hemera, the goddess of the daytime, as "Hemera the day." While the Hebrew translation could be translated as "Day the day," there is no evidence of a Canaanite goddess of daytime, supporting the Hebrew translation.

3 Codex Vacticanus: nyx nycti (ΝΥΞΝΥΚΤΙ). Translation: night (or Nyx) nightly
- Aleppo Codex: lylh llylh (**לילה ללילה**). Translations: night to night
- Leningrad Codex: layyelah lelaylah (לְיַיְלָה לְּלַיְלָֽה).
Translation: night to night
- Targum to Psalms: lêleyā lelêleyā (לֵילְיָא לְלֵילְיָא).
Translation: night to night

The Greek translation is referencing Nyx, the goddess of the nighttime, as "Nyx nightly." While the Hebrew translation could be translated as "Night to night," there is no evidence of a Canaanite goddess of daytime, supporting the Hebrew translation.

4 Codex Vacticanus: gigas (ΓΙΓΑC). Translation: Gigas
- Aleppo Codex: gbŭr (**גבור**)
- Leningrad Codex: gibbor (גִּבֹּור)
- Targum to Psalms: gibbārā (גִּבְּרָא)

In Greek mythology, Gigas was the leader of the Gigantes, an ancient tribe of demi-gods who fought the Olympian gods and lost. The Hebrew term gbŭr (גבור) is generally accepted as being an alternate spelling of the term gybŭr (גיבור), meaning "hero," or "powerful." However, the term gbŭr (גבור) is also the same as the Arabic name Jabār (الجَبَار), and the Edomite name Gbůr (٩٩٩١), the name of the constellation Orion, the giant that crosses the sky each night. The Aramaic name of the constellation was Npylyẚ (ᛝ^ᒪ^ᚢᚺ), while the later Hebrew name was Kesil (כְּסִיל), suggesting that the psalm was written in a southern Canaanite dialect earlier than the Neo-Assyrian conquest of Samaria. Based on the quotes from the Oral Torah found in Ge'ez 1st Maccabees, the Israelites believed that the descendants of Cain had worshipped the constellation. As the reference is clearly to the constellation of Orion, the common English name is used.

Psalms: Chapter 19

A psalm of David.

The Lord heard you, on the day of trouble your defense will be the name of the god of Jacob. Send help from the sanctuary, and aid out of Zion. Remember all your meat offerings, and enrich your whole burnt offering.

Separate the psalm.

Grant, if you will, and fulfill all your desires. We will celebrate in your salvation, and in the name of our god will we be praised. Lord, fulfill all your petitions. Now I know that the Lord has saved his appointed. He will hear him from the sky, his sanctified, the salvation of his right hand is mighty. Some in chariots, and some in horses, but we will glory in the name of the Lord our god.

They are overthrown and fallen, but we have risen, and have been set upright.

Lord, save the king and hear us whenever we call on you.

Psalms: Chapter 20

A psalm of David.

Lord, the king will rejoice in your strength, and in your salvation he will greatly celebrate. You have granted him the desire of his mind, and have not detained from him the request of his lips.

Separate the psalm.

For you have prevented him with blessings of goodness, and you have set on his head a crown of precious stone. He asked life of you, and you gave him length of days forever and ever. His glory is great in your salvation, and you will crown him with glory and majesty. For you will give him a blessing forever and ever, you will gladden him with joy with your countenance. For the king trusts in the Lord, and through the mercy of the Highest, he will not be moved. Let your hand be found by all your enemies, and let your right hand find all that hate you.

You will make them like a fiery oven at the time of your presence, and the Lord will trouble them in his anger, and fire will devour them. You will destroy their fruit from the earth, and their seed from among the sons of Adam. For they intended evils against you, they imagined a plan that they will by no means be able to perform. For you will make them turn their back in your latter end, you will prepare their face. Be you praised, Lord, in your strength, and we will sing and praise your mighty acts.

Psalms: Chapter 21

For the end, concerning the morning aid, a psalm of David.

God, my god, listen to me! Why have you forgotten me? The account of my transgressions is far from my salvation. My god, I cry to you during the day, but you will not hear, and at night, and it will not be considered except as foolishness by me. But you, the praise of Israel, live in a sanctuary.

Our fathers trusted in you. They trusted you, and you saved them. They cried to you and were saved. They trusted in you and were not ashamed. I am but a worm and not a man. A reproach among men, and scorn of the people. All who saw me mocked me. They spoke with their lips, and they shook their head, saying, "He trusted in the Lord. Let him save him. Let him save him because he takes pleasure in him."

For you are he who drew me out of the womb. My hope is from my mother's breasts. I have rested on you from the womb. You are my god from my mother's belly. Don't stand apart from me, for affliction is near, for there is no helper.

Many calves have surrounded me. Fat bulls have beset me. They have opened their mouth against me, as a starving and roaring lion. I am poured out like water, and all my bones are loosened. The heart in my chest has become like melting wax. My strength is dried up, like a potsherd, and my tongue is glued to my throat, and you have brought me down to the dust of death. For many dogs have surrounded me, and the assembly of the wicked doers has beset me. They pierced my hands and my feet.

They counted all my bones, and they observed and looked at me. They parted my garments among themselves and threw lots on my clothing. But you, Lord, don't remove my help too far away. Be ready for my aid. Deliver my mind from the sword, my only-begotten one from the power of the dog.

Save me from the lion's mouth, and consider my lowliness from the horn of the rhinoceros.[1] I will declare your name to my brothers, in the middle of the assembly I will sing praise to you. You who fear the Lord, praise him, and all you descendants of Jacob, praise him. Let all the descendants of Israel fear him. For he has not despised, nor been angry at the supplication of the poor, nor turned away his face from me, but when I cried to him, he heard me.

My praise is of you in the great congregation, and I will pay my vows before those who fear him. The poor will eat and be satisfied, and they will praise the Lord those who seek him, their heart will live forever. All the edges of the earth will remember and turn to the Lord, and all the families of the nations will worship before him.

For the kingdom is the Lord's, and he is the governor of the nations. All the fat ones of the earth have eaten and worshiped, and all who go down to the earth will fall down before him, and my mind also lives to him. My seed will serve him, and the generation that is coming will be reported to the Lord. They will report his righteousness to the people that will be born, whom the Lord has made.

Psalms: Chapter 21 Notes

1 Codex Vacticanus: monocerôtôn (ΜΟΝΟΚΕΡѠΤѠΝ).
Translation: Asian rhinoceros

• Septuagint Manuscript 55: monocerôton (μονοﬨόρооτον).
Translation: Asian rhinoceros

• Aleppo Codex: rmym (רמים). Translations: high (or important, loud)

• Leningrad Codex: remim (רֵמִים). Translations: high (or important, loud)

• Boharic manuscripts: monokerōtos (ΜΟΝΟΚΕΡѠΤΟС)

• Vetus Latina manuscripts: unicornton

• Targum to Psalms: rāmîn (רְמִין)

The Hebrew word is often considered a variant of the word re'eim (רְאֵים), used later in Psalms. The word re'eim was the name of an animal, although it isn't clear which animal was being referred to. It is theorized to be a reference to an extinct animal, sometimes associated with the aurochs which became extinct in the 1600s AD. The Semitic term was used for thousands of years before the Greek or Hebrew translations of Psalms were made. In Akkadian, the term was rimu (𒌷𒁯), translated as wild bull or wild donkey. In Ugaritic, it was rům (𒀖𒅆𒉈), translated as auroch or wild buffalo. In Arabic the term is riåm (ريْم), meaning onyx, or wild cattle. The meanings of the Akkadian, Ugaritic, and Hebrew terms are debated. Some scholars believe it was a generic term for a wild animal. Based on early Akkadian depictions of Asian rhinoceroses, it seems likely they were the animals intended. Monocerôtôn (Μονοκερώτων) was the ancient Greek name for the Asian rhinoceros, which, unlike the African rhinoceroses, has only one horn. In the 5th century AD, Jerome translated monocerôtôn and rmym as rhinoceros in his translation, which resulted in the Latin Vulgate. This translation is also used here.

Psalms: Chapter 22

A psalm of David.

The Lord tends me as a shepherd, and I will lack nothing. In a place of green grass, he made me live there, and he has nourished me by the water of rest. He has restored my mind, and he has guided me into the paths of righteousness, for his name's sake. Yes, even if I should walk in the middle of the shadow of Mot,[1] I will not be afraid of evils, for you are with me. Your wand and your staff have comforted me. You have prepared a table before me in the presence of those who afflict me, you have thoroughly anointed my head with oil, and your cup cheers me like the best wine. Your mercy also will follow me all the days of my life, and my residence will be in the temple of the Lord for a very long time.

Psalms: Chapter 22 Notes

1 Codex Vacticanus: thanatou (ΘΑΝΑΤΟΥ). Translation: death (or corpse, Thanatos)

• Aleppo Codex: mût (מות). Translations: death (or corpse, Mot)

• Leningrad Codex: mavet (מָ֑וֶת). Translations: death (or corpse, Mot)

• Targum to Psalms: môtā (מותא). Translations: death (or corpse)

Thanatou (θανατου) was the Greek word for death, as well as the Greek name of the god of Death, generally anglicized as Thanatos. Mt (ד— / +ﬞ) was the Canaanite god of death, as well as the word "death," generally anglicized as Mot. As the verse is referring to death as casting a shadow, it is likely a reference to the god.

Psalms: Chapter 23

A psalm of David for the Sabbath.

The earth is the Lord's and the entirety of the world, and all that live in it. He has built it on the seas, and established on it the rivers. Who will go up to the mountain of the Lord, and who will stand in his holy place?

He who is innocent in his hands and pure in his heart, who has not lifted his mind to vanity, nor sworn deceitfully to his neighbor. He will receive a blessing from the Lord, and mercy from God his savior. This is the generation of those who seek him, that seek the face of the god of Jacob.

Separate the psalm.

Lift up your gates, you princes, and be lifted forever you doors, and the king of glory will come in. Who is this King of glory? The Lord, strong and mighty, the Lord mighty in battle.

Lift up your gates, you princes, and be lifted forever you doors, and the king of glory will come in. Who is this king of glory? Lord Sabaoth![1] He is the King of glory.

Psalms: Chapter 23 Notes

1 Codex Vacticanus: cyrios tôn dynameôn (ΚΥΡΙΟCΤΩΝ ΔΥΝΑΜΕΩΝ). Translation: lord of forces

• Fragments Londinensis: (LXX U): cyrios dynameôn (ΚΥΡΙΟCΔΥΝΑΜΕΩΝ). Translation: lord forces

• Aleppo Codex: yhůh ṣbåůt (יהוה צבאות). Translations: Yhůh armies

• Leningrad Codex: Yehvah tzeva'ovt (יְהוָה צְבָאֹות). Translation: Yehvah armies

• Targum to Psalms: yeyā sebāôt (יְיָ צְבָאֹות). Translations: Yah desires

The term "ṣbåůt," used in the Aleppo Codex is the plural form of ṣbå (צבא), meaning armies in Hebrew, but "desire" or "will" in Aramaic, which resulted in the Greeks and Romans interpreting him as the Aramaean and Judean version of Dionysus and Bacchus. The Greeks transliterated ṣbåůt as Sabaoth (Σαβαώθ) but also translated it as Dionysus (Διονυσίων) or "or forces" (τῶν δυνάμεων) when translating the Septuagint, as the meaning of the name was in flux in the Judahite community at the time. The early transliterations of Sabaoth were replaced by translations of "of forces" sometime between 217 and 140 BC, indicating that Psalms was one of the later books of the Septuagint translated. It is transliterated here as the Aramaic text would have read "Lord Sabaoth" (מראך אלהא), but the definition appears to have been in flux throughout the history of the term.

The original term in the verse was probably šdy (𐎌𐎄𐎊), before the Neo-Assyrian era. This would have been impossible to translate into Neo-Assyrian cuneiform without using the term ᴵˡᵘšēdu (𒀭𒆤𒄕), which in the Neo-Assyrian era referred to a type of protective griffin. Therefore, the translator appears to have substituted the word Sebittu (𒅇𒄭𒂍). In the Old Akkadian language, the Sebittu (𒈜𒈬𒁉𒐊) had been the seven gods (planets) that ruled the sky, however, this usage had disappeared by the late bronze age, leaving only the vague concept of cosmic authority by the Neo-Babylonian era.

The related Neo-Assyrian name Sebitti (𒅇𒄭𒀸) was viewed as the god of war, which is ultimately the origin of the name of the Phrygian god of war Sabazdiôs (ϹΑΒΑΤΧΟϹ), which was later reinterpreted as Sabazios (Σαβάζιος) in the Greco-Roman era, who was viewed as the Phrygian version of Sabaoth. The merger of Sabazdiôs, Dionysus, and Sabaoth, appears to have taken place in Egypt under the rule of the last native Pharoah, Nectanebo II, who had a large number of Greek, Phrygian, and Judahite mercenaries in his army. Nectanebo II founded the cult of the Buchis Bull, which combined the cult of war god Montu, with the primordial concept of "force." The cult of Bacchus was later imported to Rome, where he was viewed as the Latin version of Dionysus, Sabaoth, and Sabazdiôs.

Psalms: Chapter 24

A psalm of David.

To you, Lord, have I lifted my mind. My god, I have trusted in you. Don't let me be confused, nor let my enemies laugh at me scornfully. For none of those who wait on you will in any way be ashamed. Let them be ashamed who transgress without cause. Show me your ways, Lord, and teach me your ways.

Lead me in your truth, and teach me, for you are God my savior, and I have waited on you all day. Remember your compassion, Lord, and your mercies, for they are from forever. Don't remember the sins of my youth, nor my sins of ignorance. Remember me according to your mercy, for your goodness sake, Lord. Good and upright is the Lord, therefore will he instruct sinners in the way.

The meek he will guide in judgment, and the meek he will teach his ways. All the ways of the Lord are mercy and truth to those who seek his covenant and his testimonies. For your name's sake, Lord, be merciful regarding my sin, for it is great. Who is the man that fears the Lord? He will instruct him in the way which he has chosen. His mind will live in prosperity, and his descendants will inherit the earth.

The Lord is the strength of those who fear him, and his covenant is to manifest truth to them. My eyes look continually to the Lord, for he will draw my feet out of the snare. Look on me, and have mercy on me, for I am an only child and poor. The plagues of my heart have been multiplied. Deliver me from my distress. Look on my affliction and my trouble, and forgive all my sins.

Look on my enemies, for they have been multiplied, and they have hated me with unjust hatred. Keep my mind, and deliver me, and let me not be ashamed, for I have trusted in you. The harmless and upright joined themselves to me, for I waited for you, Lord. Deliver Israel, God, out of all his plagues.

Psalms: Chapter 25

By David.

Judge me, Lord, for I have walked in my innocence, and I will not be moved from trusting in the Lord. Test me Lord, and try me. Purify my reins and my heart as with fire. Your mercy is before my eyes, and I am very pleased with your truth. I have not sat with the council of vanity, and will in no way enter in with transgressors. I have hated the assembly of wicked doers, and will not sit with impious men. I will wash my hands in innocent things, and circle your altar, Lord, to hear the voice of praise, and to declare all your wonderful works.

Lord, I have loved the beauty of your temple and the place of the tabernacle of your glory. Don't destroy my mind together with the impious, nor my life with bloody men in whose hands are iniquities, and their right hand is filled with bribes. I have walked in my innocence. Redeem me, and have mercy on me. My foot stands in evenness, in the congregations will I bless you, Lord.

Psalms: Chapter 26

A psalm of David before he was anointed.

The Lord is my light and my Savior. Whom will I fear? The Lord is the defender of my life. Who will I be afraid of? When evil-doers drew near against me to eat my flesh, my persecutors, and my enemies, they fainted and fell. Though an army should set itself in formation against me, my heart will not be afraid. Though war should rise against me, I am confident in this.

One thing have I asked of the Lord, this will I earnestly seek. That I should live in the temple of the Lord all the days of my life, that I should look at the fair beauty of the Lord, and survey his temple. For in the day of my plagues, he hid me in his tabernacle. He sheltered me in the secret of his tabernacle. He set me up on a rock.

Now, look, he has lifted my head over my enemies. I went around and offered in his tabernacle the sacrifice of singing. I will play on a lute and sing psalms to the Lord. Hear, Lord, my voice which I have spoken aloud. Pity me, and listen to me. My heart said to you, "I have diligently searched for your face. Your face, Lord, I will seek."

Don't turn your face away from me, don't turn away from your servant in anger. Be my helper. Don't forget me, and, God my savior, don't overlook me. For my father and my mother have forgotten me, but the Lord has taken me to himself. Teach me, Lord, in your way, and guide me on the right path, because of my enemies. Don't deliver me to those who desire to afflict me, for unjust witnesses have risen against me, and injustice has lied within herself. I believe that I will see the good things of the Lord in the land of the living.

Wait on the Lord. Be of good courage, and let your heart be strengthened. Yes, wait on the Lord.

Psalms: Chapter 27

A psalm of David.

To you, Lord, have I cried, "My God, do not be silent towards me. If you are silent towards me, I should be compared to those who go down to the pit. Listen to the voice of my supplication, when I pray to you when I lift my hands towards your sacred temple."

Don't throw away my mind with sinners, and don't destroy me with the workers of iniquity, who speak peace with their neighbors, but evils are in their hearts. Give them according to their works, and according to the iniquity of their plans, give them according to the works of their hands, render their repayment to them. Because they have not attended to the works of the Lord, even to the works of his hands, you will pull them down, and will not build them up. Blessed is the Lord, for he has listened to the voice of my petition.

The Lord is my helper and my defender, my heart has trusted in him, and I am helped, my flesh has revived, and willingly I will confess to him. The Lord is the strength of his people, and the defender and the salvation of his anointed. Save your people, and bless your inheritance, and take care of them, and lift them forever.

Psalms: Chapter 28

A psalm of David when exiting the tabernacle.

Bring to the Lord, you sons of God.[1] Bring to the Lord young rams, bring to the Lord glory and honor. Bring to the Lord the glory due to his name. Worship the Lord in his holy court.

The voice of the Lord is on the waters.

The God of glory has thundered.

The Lord is on many waters.

The voice of the Lord is mighty.

The voice of the Lord is full of majesty.

It is the voice of the Lord who breaks the cedars.

The Lord will break the cedars of Lebanon.

He will beat them small, even Lebanon itself, like a calf, and the beloved one like the young rhinoceros.[2]

There is a voice of the Lord who divides a flame of fire.

A voice of the Lord who shakes the wilderness.

The Lord will shake the wilderness of Kadesh.

The voice of the Lord strengthens the deer and will uncover the thickets.

In his temple, everyone speaks of his glory.

The Lord will live on the floodwater, and the Lord will sit as a king forever.

The Lord will give strength to his people.

The Lord will bless his people with peace.

Psalms: Chapter 28 Notes

1 Codex Vacticanus: uioe theou (ΥΙΟΙΘΕΟΥ). Translation: sons of God

- Aleppo Codex: bny ålym (בני אלים). Translations: sons of gods (or sons committing violence)
- Leningrad Codex: benei elim (בְּנֵי אֵלִים). Translation: sons of gods
- Targum to Psalms: benê ēlîm (בְּנֵי אֵלִים). Translation: sons of elim

2 Codex Vacticanus: monocerôtôn (ΜΟΝΟΚΕΡѠΤѠΝ). Translation: Asian-rhinoceros

- Septuagint manuscript 1220: monoceratôn (ΜΟΝΟΚΕΡΑΤѠΝ)
- Aleppo Codex: råmym (ראמים). Translations: oryxes (or antelopes, aurochs)
- Leningrad Codex: re'emim (רְאֵמִים). Translations: oryxes (or antelopes, aurochs)
- Sahidic manuscripts: monocerôtôs (ΜΟΝΟΚΕΡѠΤΟC)
- Targum to Psalms: rāmayā (רְמַיָא). Translation: hills (or mountains)

The word re'em was the name of an animal, although it isn't clear which animal was being referred to. It is theorized to be a reference to an extinct animal, sometimes associated with the aurochs which became extinct in the 1600s AD. The Semitic term was used for thousands of years before the Greek or Hebrew translations of Psalms were made. In Akkadian, the term was rimu (𒈨𒌋𒈣), translated as wild bull or wild donkey.

In Ugaritic, it was rům (𐎗𐎜𐎎), translated as auroch or wild buffalo. In Arabic the term is riảm (رِئْم), meaning onyx, or wild cattle. The meanings of the Akkadian, Ugaritic, and Hebrew terms are debated. Some scholars believe it was a generic term for a wild animal. Based on early Akkadian depictions of Asian rhinoceroses, it seems likely they were the animals intended. Monocerôtôn (Μονοκερώτων) was the ancient Greek name for the Asian rhinoceros, which, unlike the African rhinoceroses, has only one horn. In the 5th century AD, Jerome translated monocerôtôn and rmym as rhinoceros in his translation, which resulted in the Latin Vulgate. The Hebrew text uses the plural form, which differs from the Greek and Coptic texts, which all use a singular form. The singular form is used here as this translation is based on the Greek text.

Psalms: Chapter 29

A psalm of a song at the dedication of the palace of David.

I will praise you, Lord, for you have lifted me, and not caused my enemies to rejoice over me. The Lord my god, I cried to you, and you healed me. Lord, you have brought up my mind from Sheol, you have delivered me from among those who go down to the pit. Sing to the Lord, you saints, and give thanks for the remembrance of his holiness. For anger is in his anger, but life in his favor, weeping will wait for the evening, but joy will be in the morning.

I said in my prosperity, I will never be moved. Lord, in your good pleasure you did add strength to my beauty, but you did turn away your face, and I was troubled. To you, Lord, will I cry, and to my god will I make supplication. What profit is there in my blood, when I go down to destruction? Will the dust give praise to you? Will it declare your truth? The Lord heard and had compassion for me. The Lord has become my helper.

You have turned my mourning into joy for me. You have torn off my sackcloth, and girded me with gladness, that my glory may sing praise to you, and I may not be pierced with sorrow. Lord my god, I will give thanks to you forever.

Psalms: Chapter 30

A psalm of David, an expression of ecstasy.

Lord, I have trusted in you. Let me never be ashamed. Deliver me in your righteousness and rescue me. Incline your ear to me. Hurry to rescue me. Be for me a protecting god, and save my life like a house of refuge. For you are my strength and my refuge, and you will guide me for your name's sake, and maintain me.

You will bring me out of the snare which they have hidden for me, for you, Lord, are my defender. Into your hands, I will commit my spirit. You have redeemed me, Lord, the god of truth.[1] You have hated those who idly persist in vanities, but I have trusted in the Lord.

I will celebrate and be glad in your mercy, for you have looked on my affliction, you have saved my mind from distress. You have not trapped me in the hands of the enemy, and you have set my feet in a wide place. Pity me, Lord, for I am afflicted. My eye is troubled with indignation, my mind and my stomach.

My life is spent with grief, and my years with groaning, my strength has been weakened through poverty, and my bones are troubled. I became a reproach among all my enemies, but exceedingly so to my neighbors, and a fear to my acquaintance. They who saw me outside fled from me.

I have been forgotten like a dead man, out of mind. I have become like a broken vessel. For I heard the slander of many that lived around. When they were gathered together against me, they took counsel to take my life.

I trusted in you, Lord. I said, "You are my god. My lots are in your hands, deliver me from the hand of my enemies, and from those who persecute me. Make your face shine on your servant. Save me in your mercy. Lord, let me not be ashamed, for I have called on you. Let the impious be ashamed, and brought down to Sheol."

Let the deceitful lips become dumb, which speak iniquity against the righteous with pride and scorn. How abundant is the multitude of your goodness, Lord, which you have laid up for those who fear you! You have worked it out for those who trust in you, in the presence of the sons of Adam. You will hide them in the secret of your presence from the vexation of man. You will screen them in a tabernacle from the contradiction of tongues.

Blessed is the Lord, for he has praised his mercy in a fortified city. But I said in my extreme fear, I am thrown out from the sight of your eyes, and therefore you did listen, Lord, to the voice of my supplication when I cried to you. Love the Lord, all you, his saints, for the Lord seeks truth and renders a reward to those who deal very proudly. Be of good courage, and let your heart be strengthened, all you that hope in the Lord.

Psalms: Chapter 30 Notes

1 Codex Vacticanus: cyrie o theos tês alêthias (ΚΥΡΙΕΟ ΘΕΟϹΤΗϹΑΛΗΘΕΙΑϹ). Translation: lord the god the truth

• Dead Sea Scroll Nahal Hever Psalms: yhŭh ål åmt (יהוה אל אמת). Translations: Yhŭh god truth

• Aleppo Codex: yhŭh-ål åmt (יהוה-אל אמת). Translations: Yhŭh-god truth

• Leningrad Codex: yehvah el emet (יְהֹוָה אֵל אֱמֶת). Translation: Yehvah god truth

• Targum to Psalms: yeyā ĕlāhā qešîtā (יְיָ אֱלָהָא קְשִׁיטָא). Translation: Yah god of lamb (or money)

Psalms: Chapter 31

A psalm of instruction by David.

Blessed are those whose transgressions are forgiven, and whose sins are covered. Blessed is the man to whom the Lord will not impute sin, and whose mouth there is no guile. Because I kept silent, my bones grew old, from my crying all day. For day and night, your hand was heavy on me. I became thoroughly miserable while a thorn was fastened in me.

Separate the psalm.

I acknowledged my sin and did not hide my iniquity. I said, "I will confess my iniquity to the Lord against myself," and you forgave the impiousness of my heart.

Separate the psalm.

Therefore every holy one will pray to you in a fit time. Only in the deluge of many waters, they will not come near to him. You are my refuge from the affliction that encompasses me. My joy, to deliver me from those who have surrounded me.

Separate the psalm.

I will instruct you and guide you in this way in which you will go. I will fix my eyes on you. Don't be like the horse and mule, which have no understanding, where you must constrain their jaws with bit and curb, in case they should approach you. Many are the scourges of the sinner, but he that hopes in the Lord's mercy will circle about. Be glad in the Lord, and celebrate, you righteous, and glory, all you that are upright in heart.

Psalms: Chapter 32

A psalm of David.

Rejoice in the Lord, you righteous. Praise and become upright. Confess to the Lord on the harp. Play to him on a lute of ten strings. Sing to him a new song. Skillfully play and make a loud noise. For the word of the Lord is right, and all his works are in faithfulness. He loves mercy and judgment. The earth is full of the mercy of the Lord.

By the word of the Lord, the skies were established, and by the breath of his mouth, all their armies. He gathers the waters of the sea as if in a bottle and lays up the deeps in treasuries. Let all the earth fear the Lord, and let all that live in the world be moved because of him. For he spoke, and they were made, and he commanded, and they were created.

The Lord frustrates the counsels of the nations, and he brings to nothing also the reasoning of the peoples and brings to nothing the counsels of princes. But the counsel of the Lord endures forever, the thoughts of his heart from generation to generation. Blessed is the nation whose god is the Lord, and the people whom he has chosen for his own inheritance.

The Lord looks out of the sky. He sees all the sons of Adam. He looks from his prepared habitation on all the residents on the earth who fashioned their hearts individually, and who understand all their works. A king is not saved because of a great army, and Orion will not be delivered by the greatness of his strength. A horse is vain for safety, neither will he be delivered by the greatness of his power.

Look, the eyes of the Lord are on those who fear him, those who hope in his mercy to deliver their minds from death, and to keep them alive in famine. Our mind waits on the Lord, for he is our helper and defender. For our heart will rejoice in him, and we have trusted in his holy name. Let your mercy, Lord, be on us, as we have trusted in you.

Psalms: Chapter 33

A psalm of David, when he changed his attitude before Abimelech, and he let him go, and he departed.

I will bless the Lord at all times. His praise will be continually in my mouth. My mind will be praised in the Lord. Let the meek hear, and rejoice. Praise the Lord with me, and let us praise his name together. I searched for the Lord diligently, and he listened to me and delivered me from all my neighbors.

Draw near to him and be enlightened, and your faces will not by any means be ashamed. This poor man cried, and the Lord listened to him and delivered him out of all his plagues. The messenger of the lord[1] will camp around those who fear him and will deliver them.

Taste and see that the Lord is good. Blessed is the man who hopes in him. Fear the Lord, all you, his saints, for there is no lack to those who fear him. The rich have become poor and hungry, but those who seek the Lord diligently will not lack any good thing.

Separate the psalm.

Come, you children, listen to me, and I will teach you to fear the Lord. What man is there that desires life, loving to see good days? Keep your tongue from evil, and your lips from speaking guile. Turn away from evil, and do good, and seek peace, and pursue it.

The eyes of the Lord are over the righteous, and his ears are open to their prayer, but the face of the Lord is against those who do evil, to destroy their memorial from the earth. The righteous cried, and the Lord listened to them and delivered them out of all their plagues.

The Lord is near to the broken in heart and will save the lowly in spirit. Many are the plagues of the righteous, but out of them, all the Lord will deliver them. He keeps all their bones, not one of them will be broken. The death of sinners is evil, and those who hate righteousness will go wrong. The Lord will redeem the minds of his servants: and none of those who trust in him will go wrong.

Psalms: Chapter 33 Notes

1 Codex Vaticanus: angelos cyriou (ⲀⲅⲅⲈⲗⲟⲥⲔⲨⲣⲓⲟⲨ). Translation: messenger lord

• Aleppo Codex: mlåk-yhŭh (מלאך-יהוה). Translations: messenger-Yhŭh

• Leningrad Codex: mal'ach-yehvah (מַלְאַךְ־יְהֹוָה). Translation: messenger-Yehvah

• Targum to Psalms: malăkā dayyā (מַלְאֲכָא דַיְיָ). Translation: messenger of Yah

The Greek angelos cyriou (ἄγγελοσ κυρίου) is often translated as "angel of the lord," however, that would have been angelos tou Cyriou (ἄγγελοσ του κυρίου). The Hebrew mal'ach Yehovah (מַלְאַךְ יְהֹוָה) translates as "angel Yahweh," however, that term was not in the Aramaic texts, or the Greeks would have translated it as angelos Iaw (ἄγγελοσ Ιαω). The term the Greeks translated as "Angel Lord," appears to be Malakbel, the sun-god, and messenger-god of the Aramaic (Syrian) religion, however, it is unclear when Malakbel began being worshiped in Aram, or if the earliest version was a solar deity, however, the name indicates that Malakbel was always a messenger lord.

Psalms: Chapter 34

A psalm of David.

Judge, Lord, those who injure me. Fight against those who fight against me. Take hold of a shield and a buckler and rise to help me. Bring out a sword, and block the path of those who persecute me. Tell my mind, "I am your salvation."

Let those who seek my mind be ashamed and confused. Let those who plan evils against me be turned back and put to shame. Let them be like dust in the wind, with a messenger of the lord afflicting them. Let their way be dark and slippery, with a messenger of the lord persecuting them.

Without cause, they have hidden for me their destructive snare. Without a cause, they have insulted my mind. Let a snare which they don't know come on them, and the trap which they hid take them, and let them fall into the very same snare.

But my mind will celebrate in the Lord. It will delight in his salvation. All my bones will say, "Lord, who is like you? Delivering the poor out of the hand of those who are stronger than he, yes, the poor and needy one from those who spoil him."

Unjust witnesses arose and asked me of things I knew not. They rewarded me evil for good and bereaved my mind. But I, when they troubled me, put on sackcloth, and humiliated my mind with fasting, and my prayer will return to my own bosom. I behaved agreeably towards them as if it had been our neighbor or brother. I humiliated myself like one mourning and depressed.

Yet they rejoiced against me, and many plagues were brought against me, and I did not know it. They were scattered but did not repent. They tempted me, they sneered at me most contemptuously, and they gnashed their teeth at me.

Lord, when will you see me? Save my mind from their plans, my only-begotten one, from the lions. I will give thanks to you even in a great congregation, in an abundant people I will praise you. Don't let those who are my enemies without a cause rejoice against me, who hate me for nothing, and wink with their eyes. For to me, they spoke peaceably but imagined deceits in their anger. They opened wide their mouth at me. They said, "Aha, aha, our eyes have seen it."

You have seen it, Lord, don't keep silent Lord, don't withdraw yourself from me. Awake, Lord, and attend to my judgment, even to my cause, my god, and my lord. Judge me, Lord, according to your righteousness, Lord my god, and let them not rejoice against me. Don't let them say in their hearts, "Aha, aha, it is pleasing to our mind," nor let them say, "We have devoured him."

Let them be confused and ashamed together, those who rejoice at my plagues, and let them be clothed with shame and confusion that speaks great swelling words against me. Let those who rejoice in my righteousness celebrate and be glad, and let them say continually, "Lord be praised," who desire the peace of his servant. My tongue will meditate on your righteousness, and your praise all day.

Psalms: Chapter 35

For the end, by David the servant of the Lord.

The transgressor who sins, says within himself, that there is no fear of God before his eyes. For he has dealt craftily before him, to discover his iniquity and hate it. The words of his mouth are transgression and deceit, he is not inclined to understand how to do good.

He devises iniquity on his bed, he gives himself to every evil way and does not abhor evil. Lord, your mercy is in the sky, and your truth reaches up to the clouds. Your righteousness is like the vast mountains of God, your judgments are like the great deep. Lord, you will preserve men and beasts. How you have multiplied your mercy, God! So the children of men will trust in the shelter of your wings.

They will be intoxicated with the oil of your house, and you will cause them to drink the full stream of your delights. For in you is the fountain of life, and in your light we see light. Extend your mercy to those who know you, and your righteousness to the upright in heart. Don't let the foot of pride come against me, and don't let the hand of sinners move me. There have all the workers of iniquity fallen. They are thrown out, and will not be able to stand.

Psalms: Chapter 36

A psalm of David.

Don't concern yourself because of evil-doers, nor envy those who do iniquity. For they will soon be withered like the grass, and will soon fall away like the green plants. Hope in the Lord, and do good, and live on the land, and you will be fed with the wealth of it.

Delight yourself in the Lord, and he will grant you the requests of your heart. Confess your way to the Lord, and trust in him, and he will bring it to pass. He will bring out your righteousness as the light, and your judgment like the noonday.

Submit yourself to the Lord, and supplicate to him. Don't concern yourself because of him who prospers in his way, at the man that does unlawful deeds. Ease from anger, and forget the anger. Don't concern yourself and do evil, for evildoers will be destroyed, but those who wait on the Lord will inherit the land. In just a little while, the sinner will no longer exist, and you will search for his home, and will not find it. But the meek will inherit the earth and will delight themselves in the abundance of peace.

The sinner will watch for the righteous, and gnash his teeth on him. But the Lord will laugh at him, for he foresees that his day will come. Sinners have drawn their swords, they have bent their bow, to throw down the poor and needy, and to kill the upright in heart.

Let their sword enter into their own heart, and their bows be broken. A little is better to the righteous than an abundant wealth to sinners. For the arms of sinners will be broken, but the Lord supports the righteous. The Lord knows the ways of the perfect, and their inheritance will be forever. They will not be ashamed in an evil time, and in days of famine, they will be satisfied.

For the sinners will perish, and the enemies of the Lord at the moment of their being honored and praised have completely vanished like smoke. The sinner borrows, and will not pay again, but the righteous has compassion and gives.

For those who bless him will inherit the earth, and those who curse him will be annihilated. The steps of a man are rightly ordered by the Lord, and he will take pleasure in his way. When he falls, he will not be ruined, for the Lord supports his hand. I was once young, indeed I am now old, yet I have not seen the righteous forgotten, nor his descendants seeking bread. He is merciful and lends continually, and his descendants will be a blessing.

Turn aside from evil, and do good, and live forever. The Lord loves judgment, and will not forget his saints.

They will be preserved forever, the blameless will be cleared in judgment, but the descendants of the impious will be annihilated. But the righteous will inherit the earth, and live on it forever.

The mouth of the righteous will meditate wisdom, and his tongue will speak of judgment. The law of his god is in his heart, and his steps will not be tripped up. The sinner watches the righteous and seeks to kill him. The Lord will not leave him in his hands, nor by any means condemn him when he is judged.

Wait on the Lord, and follow his ways, and he will praise you to inherit the land when the wicked are destroyed, you will see it. I saw the impious very highly exalting himself, and lifting himself like the cedars of Lebanon. Yet I returned and saw he was no more. I searched for him, but his home was not found.

Maintain innocence, and look upright, for there is a remnant to the peaceful man. The transgressors will be annihilated together, and the remnants of the impious will be annihilated. The salvation of the righteous is from the Lord, and he is their defender in the time of affliction. The Lord will help them, and deliver them, and he will rescue them from sinners, and save them because they have trusted in him.

Psalms: Chapter 37

A psalm of David for remembrance concerning the Sabbath.

Lord, don't rebuke me in your anger, nor punish me in your anger. For your weapons are fixed on me, and you have pressed your hand heavily on me. For there is no health in my flesh because of your anger. There is no peace to my bones because of my sins.

My transgressions have gone over my head, and they have pressed heavily on me like a weighty burden. My bruises have become noisome and corrupt, because of my foolishness. I have been wretched and bowed down continually, and I went with a mourning countenance all day.

For my mind is filled with mocking, and there is no health in my flesh. I have been afflicted and brought down exceedingly, and I have roared for the groaning of my heart. But all my desire is before you, and my groaning is not hidden from you. My heart is troubled, my strength has failed me, and the light of my eyes is not with me.

My friends and my neighbors drew near before me and stood still, and my nearest family stood far away. While they pressed hard on me, those who wanted my mind, and those who wanted my injury, spoke vanities and devised lies all day. But I, like a deaf man, did not hear, and like a dumb man, did not open my mouth. I was like a man that does not hear, and who has no argument in his mouth.

For I trusted in you, Lord, and you will hear, "Lord, my god."

I said, "In case my enemies rejoice against me, for when my feet were moved, they boasted against me."

I am ready for scourges, and my grief is continually before me. For I will declare my iniquity, and be distressed for my sin. But my enemies live and are mightier than I, and those who hate me unjustly are multiplied. They who reward evil for good slandered me because I followed righteousness.

Don't forget me, Lord my god. Don't leave me. Draw near and help, Lord of my salvation.

Psalms: Chapter 38

For the end. To Idithun. A song of David.

I said, "I will pay attention to my ways, so I don't sin with my tongue. I set a guard on my mouth, while the sinner stood in my presence."

I was dumb and humiliated myself, and kept silent from good words, and my grief was renewed. My heart grew hot within me, and a fire would kindle in my meditation. I said with my tongue, "Lord, let me know my end, and the number of my days, what it is, that I may know what I lack. Look, you have made my days a long span, and my existence is as nothing before you, no, every man living is altogether vanity."

Separate the psalm.

Certainly, a man walks in an image. He is disquieted and vain. He lays up treasures and doesn't know for whom he will gather them. Now, what is my expectation? Is it not the Lord? My ground of hope is with you.

Separate the psalm.

Deliver me from all my transgressions, you have made me a reproach to the foolish. I was made dumb and did not open my mouth, for you are he that made me. Remove your scourges from me. I have fainted because of the strength of your hand. You punish man with rebukes for iniquity, and you make his life waste away like a spider's web. No, every man is disquieted and vain.

Separate the psalm.

Lord, listen to my prayer and my supplication. Attend to my tears, and do not be silent, for I am a visitor to the land, and an alien, as all my fathers were. Spare me, that I may be refreshed before I leave, and be no more.

Psalms: Chapter 39

A psalm of David.

I waited patiently for the Lord, and he paid attention to me and listened to my supplication. He brought me up out of a pit of misery, and from the miry clay, and he set my feet on a rock and ordered my actions correctly. He put a new song into my mouth, even a hymn to our god, many will see it, and fear, and hope in the Lord.

Blessed is the man whose hope is in the name of the Lord, and who has not regarded vanities and false frenzies. Lord my god, you have multiplied your wonderful works, and in your thoughts, none will be compared to you. I declared and spoke of them, and they exceeded in numbers.

Sacrifice and offering you would not accept, as a body you had prepared for me, and the whole burnt offering and sacrifice for sin you did not require.

Then I said, "Look, I have come," in the volume of the book that is written concerning me. I desired to do your will, my god, and keep your law in my heart. I have preached righteousness in the great congregation. Look! I will not refrain my lips. Lord, you know my righteousness.

I have not hidden your truth within my heart, and I have declared your salvation. I have not hidden your mercy and your truth from the great congregation. But you, Lord, don't remove your compassion far from me. Your mercy and your truth have helped me continually, for innumerable evils have surrounded me, and my transgressions have taken hold of me, and I could not see. They are multiplied more than the hairs of my head, and my heart has failed me.

Be pleased, Lord, to deliver to me. Lord, draw near to help me. Let those who seek my mind, to destroy it, be ashamed and confused together, let those who wish me evil be turned backward and put to shame. Let those who say to me, "Aha, aha, quickly receive shame for their reward."

Let all those who seek you, Lord, celebrate and rejoice in you, and let those who love your salvation say continually, "Lord be praised. I am but poor and needy, and the Lord will take care of me."

You are my helper, and my defender, my god, don't delay.

Psalms: Chapter 40

A psalm of David.

Blessed is the man who thinks about the poor and needy. The Lord will deliver him on an evil day. May the Lord preserve him and keep him alive, and bless him on the earth, and not deliver him into the hands of his enemy. May the Lord help him on the bed of his pain, you have made all his bed in his sickness.

I said, "Lord, have mercy on me, heal my mind, for I have sinned against you. My enemies have spoken evil against me, saying, "When will he die, and his name perish? If he came to see me, his heart spoke vainly, he gathered iniquity to himself, he went out and spoke in the same manner." All my enemies whispered against me, against me they devised my injury. They denounced a wicked word against me, saying, "Now that he lies, will he not rise again?"

For even the man of my peace, in whom I trusted, who ate my bread, lifted his heel against me. But you, Lord, have compassion on me and raise me, and I will requite them. By this, I know that you have delighted in me because my enemy will not rejoice over me. But you did help me because of my innocence and have established me before you forever. Blessed is the Lord, the god in Israel from forever, and to forever. So be it, so be it.

Psalms: Chapter 41

A psalm for instruction, for the sons of Korah.

As the deer earnestly desires the fountains of water, so my mind earnestly longs for you, God. My mind has thirsted for the living God. When will I come and appear before God? My tears have been bread for me day and night, while they asked me daily, "Where is your god?"

I remembered these things, and poured out my mind in me, for I will go to the place of your wondrous tabernacle, to the temple of God,[1] with a voice of celebration and thanksgiving and of the sound of those who keep the festival.

Why are you very sad, my mind? Why do you trouble me? Hope in God, for I will give thanks to him, as he is the salvation of my countenance.

My god, my mind has been troubled within me. Why I will remember you from the land of Jordan, and of the Hermonites[2] from Mount Misor.[3]

Deep calls to deep at the voice of your cataracts. All your billows and your waves have gone over me. By day the Lord will command his mercy, and manifest it by night, with me is a prayer to the god of my life. I will say to God, "You are my helper. Why have you forgotten me? Why do I become sad, while the enemy oppresses me? While my bones were breaking, those who afflicted me and insulted me. While they said to me daily, 'Where is your God?'"

Why are you very sad, my mind? Why do you trouble me? Hope in God. I will give thanks to him, and he is the health of my countenance and my god.

Psalms: Chapter 41 Notes

1 Codex Vacticanus: oecou tou theou (ΟΙΚΟΥΤΟΥΘΕΟΥ). Translation: temple (or sanctuary) of the god

* Aleppo Codex: byt ålhym (בית אלהים). Translations: house (or temple, palace) Elohim

* Leningrad Codex: beit elohim (בֵּית אֱלֹהִים). Translation: house (or temple, palace) Elohim

* Targum to Psalms: bêt mûqedšā dayyā (בֵּית מוּקְדְשָׁא דַיְיָ). Translation: house that is sacred to Yah

2 Codex Vacticanus: Ermôniim (ЄΡΜΩΝΙΙΜ)

* Aleppo Codex: hrmûnym (חרמונים). Translations: Hermonites (people from Mount Hermon)

* Leningrad Codex: hermônîm (חֶרְמוֹנִים). Translation: Hermonites (people from Mount Hermon)

* Oxford pericopes (VL111): hermoni

* Bohairic manuscripts: ēermonim (ΗЄΡΜΟΝΙΜ)

* Sahidic manuscripts: ēermon (ΗЄΡΜΟΝ)

* Targum to Psalms: hermônî (חֶרְמוֹנִי)

All the surviving variants of this name support it being associated with Mount Hermon. King David is recorded as building a palace on Mount Hermon, supporting this reading. The sect associated with Mount Hermon in ancient times was the Enochians, who believed the watchers descended from the sky and landed on Mount Hermon.

3 Codex Vaticanus: arous microu (ΟΡΟΥϹΜΙΚΡΟΥ). Translation: mount small (or short, insignificant)

• Aleppo Codex: hr mṣôr (חר מצער). Translations: mount minimum (or Misor)

• Leningrad Codex: har mitz'ar (הַר מִצְעָר). Translation: mount minimum

• Targum to Psalms: ṭûrā desînay (טוּרָא דְסִינַי). Translation: mount of Sinai

Based on Middle Egyptian records of the Amorite occupation of Canaan, and the Old Babylonian epic of Gilgamesh, it's possible that this was a reference to Mount Carmel, which is a flat table-like mountain range, that runs straight southeast across northern Israel into the West Bank. The Middle Egyptian records link the Carmel mountain range and the Hermon Mountain range politically under the rule of the Amorites, along with the Jazreel Valley in between them. In the Old Babylonian Epic of Gilgamesh, he ventured to the Cedar Forest, accepted as a reference to the Jazreel Valley, where he and his friend Enkidu killed the Huwawa (𒄷𒉿𒉿) giant. In the earlier Neo-Sumerian version of tales of Bilgamesh, the Huúú (𒄷𒅊𒅊) monster was in the Zagros mountains, however, during the Old Babylonian era, the story changed to the Cedar Forest, and the monster became a giant. This suggests the story was reformatted during the Old Babylonian Empire to mythologize the conquest of the Cedar Forest region by the Babylonian Empire. The giant in the sky, Orion, was the god of the Enochians, who threw some of the stars out of the sky each October when the Earth moves through the debris of Haley's comet, and the Orionid meteor storm appears to fall from Orion's upstretched arm.

The term appears to have been misunderstood by the Greeks, who translated it as microu (μικρου), meaning small, presumably from the similar-sounding word mitz'ar (מִזְעָר). The term mṣôr (מצער), was the name of the Canaanite god Misor, the bother of Sydyk. Misor (𐤑𐤃𐤒) was also the word meaning "straight" in Canaanite. The location of the "small mountain" is debated today. Mount Hermon is a range extending 70 km from north to south and has three peaks of similar height. One theory is that the small mountain was one of the peaks.

Based on Middle Egyptian records of the Amorite occupation of Canaan, and the Old Babylonian epic of Gilgamesh, this appears to have been a reference to Mount Carmel, which is a flat table-like mountain range, that runs straight southeast across northern Israel into the West Bank. The Middle Egyptian records link the Carmel mountain range and the Hermon Mountain range politically under the rule of the Amorites, along with the Jazreel Valley in between them. In the Old Babylonian Epic of Gilgamesh, he ventured to the Cedar Forest, accepted as a reference to the

Jezreel Valley, where he and his friend Enkidu killed the Huwawa (𒄷𒉿𒉿) giant.

In the earlier Neo-Sumerian version of tales of Bilgamesh, the Ḫuúú (𒄷𒄷𒄷) monster was in the Zagros mountains, however, during the Old Babylonian era, the story changed to the Cedar Forest, and the monster became a giant. This suggests the story was reformatted during the Old Babylonian Empire to mythologize the conquest of the Cedar Forest region by the Babylonian Empire. The giant in the sky, Orion, was the god of the Enochians, who threw some of the stars out of the sky each October. In Enochian literature, these fallen stars were called the ôyryn (ʒ^ʝ^ʊ) in the surviving Aramaic texts, a word which means either 'watchers,' or 'guardians.' During the Akkadian era, Orion and Sagittarius were the two guardians of the sky, which is likely where the names ôyryn (ʒ^ʝ^ʊ) and Ôriôn (Ὠρίων) originated. During the Neo-Sumerian era, the Amorites rebelled from the rule of the Ur III dynasty, and Saggitarius became associated with their dominant god, Rasheph. Later, during the Old Babylonian era, Sagittarius became associated with the Nergal, the Babylonian ruler of the underworld, indicating that Saggitarius was very low on the western horizon, and no longer one of the guardians of the sky.

Psalms: Chapter 42

A psalm of David.

Judge me, God, and plead my cause, against an impious nation, and deliver me from the unjust and cunning man. For you, God, are my strength, why have you thrown me off? Why do I become sad, while the enemy oppresses me?

You sent out your light and your truth and they have led me, and brought me to your holy mountain, and your tabernacles. I will go into the altar of God, to God who gladdens my youth. I will give thanks to you on the harp, God, my God. Why are you very sad, my mind? Why do you trouble me? Hope in God, and I will give thanks to him, who is the health of my countenance, and my god.

Psalms: Chapter 43

A psalm for understanding, for the sons of Korah.

God, we have heard with our ears, our fathers have told us, the work which you worked in their days, in the days of old. Your hand completely destroyed the foreigner, and you routed them. You afflicted the nations, and drove them out. They did not inherit the land by their own sword, and their own arm did not deliver them, but your right hand, and your arm, and the light of your countenance, because you were very pleased in them.

You are indeed my king and my god, who command deliverance for Jacob. Through you we will suppress our enemies, and in your name will we bring to nothing those who rise up against us. I will not trust in my bow, and my sword will not save me. For you have saved us from those who afflicted us, and have put to shame those who hated us. God will be praised all day, and to your name will we give thanks forever.

Separate the psalm.

Now you have abandoned away and shamed us. You will not go out with our armies. You have turned us back before our enemies, and those who hated us spoiled for themselves. You made us like sheep for meat, and you scattered us among the nations. You have sold your people without price, and there was no profit from their exchange. You have made us an insult among our neighbors, a scorn and derision to those who are around us.

You have made us a proverb among the nations, a shaking of the head among the nations. All the day my shame is before me, and the confusion of my face has covered me, because of the voice of the slanderer and reviler. Because of the enemy and avenger. All these things have come on us, but we have not forgotten you, neither have we dealt unrighteously in your covenant.

Our heart has not gone back, but you have turned aside our paths from your way. For you have laid us low in a place of affliction, and the shadow of death has covered us. If we have forgotten the name of our god, and if we have spread out our hands to a foreign god, will God not learn these things? He knows the secrets of the heart.

For your sake, we are killed all day long. We are counted as sheep for the slaughter. Awake! Why do you sleep, Lord? Rise, and do not throw us away forever. Why do you turn your face away, and forget our poverty and our affliction? For our mind has been brought down to the dust. Our belly has clung to the earth.

Rise, Lord, help us and redeem us for your name's sake.

Psalms: Chapter 44

For the end, for alternate, by the sons of Korah. For instruction, a song concerning the beloved.

My heart has spoken a good matter. I declare my works to the king. My tongue is the pen of a quick writer. You are more beautiful than the sons of Adam, grace has been shed forth on your lips, and therefore God has blessed you forever. Gird your sword on your thigh Orion,[1] in your handsomeness, and your beauty, and bend your bow, and prosper, and reign, because of truth and meekness and righteousness, and your right hand will guide you wonderfully.

Your weapons are sharpened Orion, and nations throw themselves down under you in the heart of the king's enemies. Your throne, God, is forever and ever. The scepter of your kingdom is a scepter of righteousness. You have loved righteousness and hated iniquity. Therefore god, your god has anointed you with the oil of gladness beyond your fellows.

Myrrh, stacte, and cassia are exhaled from your garments, and out of the ivory palaces, with which kings' daughters have gladdened you for your honor. The queen stood by on your right hand, clothed in clothing worked with gold, and arrayed in various colors. Hear, daughter, and see, and incline your ear, and forget also your people, and your father's house.

Because the king has desired your beauty, for he is your lord. The daughter of Tyre[2] will adore him with gifts. The rich of the people of the land will supplicate your face.

All her glory, of the daughter of the king of Heshbon, robed in golden fringed garments, in embroidery. Virgins will be brought to the king after her. Her fellows will be brought to you. They will be brought with gladness and celebration. They will be led to the king's temple.

Instead of your fathers, children are born to you. You will make them princes over all the earth. They will make mention of your name from generation to generation. Therefore the nations will give thanks to you forever and ever.

Psalms: Chapter 44 Notes

1 Codex Vacticanus: dynate (ΔΥΝΑΤΕ). Translation: strong

• Aleppo Codex: gbŭr (גבור). Translations: hero (or strong, powerful, brave)

• Leningrad Codex: gibbôr (גִּבּוֹר). Translation: hero (or strong, powerful, brave)

• Targum to Psalms: gibbārā (גִּבְּרָא). Translation: man (or husband)

Based on the other translation of gbŭr (גבור) as gigas (γιγασ) in chapter 18, which is a reference to the constellation Orion, that interpretation is used here.

2 Codex Vacticanus: Tyrou (ΤΥΡΟΥ). Translation: Tyre
- Aleppo Codex: sr (צר). Translations: Tyre (or rock)
- Leningrad Codex: tzor (צֹר). Translation: Tyre (or rock)
- Targum to Psalms: ṣûr (צור). Translation: Tyre

Psalms: Chapter 45

For the end, for the sons of Korah. A psalm concerning secret things.

God is our refuge and strength, a help in the plagues that have come heavily on us. Therefore we will not fear when the earth is troubled, and the mountains are thrown into the depths of the seas. Their waters have roared and been troubled, the mountains have been troubled by his might.

Separate the psalm.

The flowing of the river gladdens the city of God, the Highest has sanctified his tabernacle. God is in the middle of her. She will not be moved. God will help her with his attitude. The nations were troubled, the kingdoms tottered, and he spoke his voice, the earth shook. Lord Sabaoth is with us, the god of Jacob is our helper.

Separate the psalm.

Come, and look at the works of the Lord, what wonders he has achieved on the earth. Putting an end to wars as for the edges of the earth. He will crush the bow, break in pieces the weapon, and burn the bucklers with fire. Be still, and know that I am God. I will be praised among the nations, I will be praised in the earth.

Lord Sabaoth is with us! The God of Jacob is our helper.

Psalms: Chapter 46

A psalm for the sons of Korah.

Clap your hands, all you nations. Shout to God with a voice of celebration. For the Highest lord is terrible. He is a great king over all the earth. He has subdued the peoples under us, and the nations under our feet. He has chosen out his inheritance for us, the beauty of Jacob which he loved.

Separate the psalm.

God has gone up with a shout, Lord with the sound of a trumpet. Sing praises to our God! Sing praises! Sing praises to our king! Sing praises. For God is the king of all the earth. Sing praises with understanding. God reigns over the nations. God sits on the throne of his holiness. The rulers of the people are assembled with the god of Abraham. Those of God's mighty of the earth[1] have been praised.

Psalms: Chapter 46 Notes

1 Codex Vacticanus: theou hoe crataeoe tês gês (ΘΕΟΥ ΟΙ ΚΡΑΤΑΙΟΙ ΤΗϹ ΓΗϹ). Translation: god the mighties of the earth

- Aleppo Codex: lålhym mgny-års (לאלהים מגני-ארץ).
Translations: the gods shields-earth

- Leningrad Codex: lelohim maginnei-eretz (לֵאלֹהִים מָגִנֵּי־אֶרֶץ). Translation: the gods shields-earth
- Targum to Psalms: yeyā terêsê arôā (יְיָ תְּרֵיסֵי אַרְעָא). Translation: Yah the shield of land

Psalms: Chapter 47

A psalm of a song for the sons of Korah on the second day of the week.

Great is the Lord, and greatly to be praised in the city of our god, in his holy mountain. The city of the great king is well planted on the mountains of Zion, with the joy of the whole earth, on the sides of the north. God is known in her palaces when he undertakes to help her. For, look the kings of the earth were assembled, they came together.

They saw, and so they wondered, and they were troubled, and they were moved. Trembling took hold of them. There were the pangs as of a woman in labor. You will break the ships of Tharsis[1] with a vehement wind. As we have heard, so have we also seen, in the city of Lord Sabaoth, in the city of our god. God has founded it forever.

Separate the psalm.

We have thought of your mercy, God, in the middle of your people. According to your name God, so is your praise to the edges of the earth. Your right hand is full of righteousness. Let Mount Zion rejoice, let the daughters of Judah celebrate, because of your judgments, Lord. Go around Zion, and circle her. Describe her towers. Observe her strength, and her palaces, that you may tell the next generation.

For this is our God forever and ever. He will be our guide forever.

Psalms: Chapter 47 Notes

1 Codex Vacticanus: Tharsis (ӨΛΡϲιϲ)

* Aleppo Codex: tršyš (תרשיש)
* Leningrad Codex: tarshish (תַּרְשִׁישׁ)
* Targum to Psalms: ṭarsîs (טָרְסִיס)

This civilization was mentioned in several ancient documents, including the inscriptions of Esarhaddon from Assyria and the Nora Stone from Phoenicia. Based on the various descriptions of the land in Phoenician, Hebrew, and Assyrian sources, Tharsis was in the Mediterranean or the Atlantic Ocean, somewhere west of Malta. The Greek historian Herodotus recorded that at his time, circa 450 BC, the city of Tartessos was a major trading center, past the "Pillars of Herakles" or in modern terms, outside the Mediterranean, on the Atlantic Coast somewhere. This is generally considered to be the same civilization, implying it existed from at least 1000 BC to at least 450 BC. The dominant theory of the past century is that it was the "Tartessos" culture of southwest Spain.

The name Tartessos was adopted from Greek geography by modern archaeologists, and it is unclear if they called their civilization something that sounded like Tartessos. Several ancient ruins and inscriptions have been found in the area, using the Phoenician script, but written in a language dubbed

"Tartessian." The records of the Hebrews, Phoenicians, and Assyrians all record that Tarshiysh was a metal-rich land, which exported large amounts of silver, iron, tin, and other metals. The records of the ancient Greeks reported the same about Tartessos. Modern archaeology in the region around Cadiz does support that this was a metal exporting nation, and therefore the evidence is strongly supportive of this being the civilization referred to in the Septuagint. Several other locations have historically been proposed as the potential location of Tharsis, including Sardinia, Italy, Britain, West Africa, and Southern India. Most of these proposals predated the discovery of the Assyrian and Phoenician records of Tharsis, however, the proposal that Tharsis was in Britain is still supported by some, as the British were also exporting tin to the Phoenicians at the time.

Psalms: Chapter 48

A psalm for the sons of Korah.

Hear these words, all you nations. Listen, all you that live on the earth, both the earth-born and sons of great men, the rich and poor man together. My mouth will speak of wisdom, and the meditation of my heart will bring forth understanding. I will incline my ear to a parable, and I will play my riddle on the harp.

Why will I be afraid on the evil day? The iniquity of my heel will circle me. They that trust in their strength, boast about themselves of the multitude of their wealth. A brother does not redeem, will a man redeem? He will not give to God a ransom for himself, or the price of the redemption of his mind, though he labors forever, and lives to the end so that he should not see corruption.

When he sees wise men dying, the fool and the senseless one will perish together, and they will leave their wealth to strangers. Their sepulchers are their houses forever, even their tabernacles to all generations. They have called their lands after their names.

Man being in honor, does not understand. He is compared to the senseless livestock and those like them. This, their way, is an offense to them. Yet afterward, men will commend their sayings.

Separate the psalm.

They have laid them as sheep in Sheol. Mot[1] will feed on them, and the upright will have dominion over them in the morning, and their help will fail in Sheol from their glory. But God will deliver my mind from the hand of Sheol[2] when he will receive me.

Separate the psalm.

Don't be afraid when a man is enriched, and when the glory of his house is increased. For he will take nothing when he dies, neither will his glory descend with him. For his mind will be blessed in his life. He will give thanks to you when you do well to him. Yet he will go into the generation of his fathers, he will never see light. Man is honored, yet does not understand He is compared to the senseless livestock and is like them.

Psalms: Chapter 48 Notes

1 Codex Vacticanus: thanatos (ΘΑΝΑΤΟϹ). Translation: Thanatos (or death, corpse)

- Aleppo Codex: mŭt (מות). Translation: Mot (or death)
- Leningrad Codex: mavet (מָוֶת). Translation: death
- Targum to Psalms: môtā (מוֹתָא). Translation: death

The Masoretic word mŭt (מות) is generally assumed to be a spelling error of mŭŭt (מוות), meaning "death," however, as the Sons of Korah were driven out of the temple during the reforms of Hezekiah and Josiah, it must be assumed that the psalm must have been composed in Judahite, using the older Canaanite script. Mot spelled variously as Mūtu (⊢<) in Akkadian cuneiform, Mǔt (𓏠𓂝𓆑) in Egyptian, Mata (𓈖𓏠𓆑) in Kushite, Mt (𐎊—) in Ugaritic, Mt (𐤕𐤌) in Phoenician, Mǔtå (𐡌𐡅𐡕𐡀) in Aramaic, Mmt (ⵎⵎⵜ) in Central Atlas Tamazight, Mǔtå (ܡܘܬܐ) in Syriac, Mout (ⲙⲟⲩⲧ) in Coptic, Mata (𐦠𐦢) in Meroitic, Maǔt (موت) in Arabic, and Mot (ሞት) in Ge'ez, was and is the word for death.

In Canaan, he was also the God of death, similar to the Greek Thanatos. In the Ugaritic Texts, from the late bronze age, Mot killed Baal Hadad, the lord of thunder, however, Baal escaped the afterlife with the help of Shapash, the goddess of justice. Mot is well documented among the Canaanite gods, in both the Ugaritic Texts and the writings of Sanchuniathon. In the Canaanite religion, Mot was the son of El (God), and the ruler of the "pit" called Mirey, where the dead resided. In the Israelite texts, Mot was treated like the angel of death, instead of the god of death, later interpreted as the Thanatos, the angel of Death in the early Christian era.

2 Codex Vacticanus: chiros hadou (χειροσ αιδου). Translation: hand of Hades (or underworld)

• Aleppo Codex: myd-šåůl (מִיד-שְׁאוּל). Translation: hand of Sheol

• Leningrad Codex: miyyad-she'ovl (מִיד־שְׁאוֹל). Translation: hand of Sheol (or grave)

• Targum to Psalms: dîn gēhinām (דִּין גֵהִנָּם). Translation: judgment of Gehenna

Sheol was a personification of the underworld, similar to the Greek Hades.

Psalms: Chapter 49

A Psalm for Asaph.

El, Lord of the gods,[1] has spoken and called the earth from the rising of the sun to its setting. Out of Zion comes the excellence of his beauty. Our god will come manifestly, and will not keep silent, a fire will be started before him, and around him, there will be a very great storm. He will summon the sky above, and the earth, that he may judge his people. Assemble to him you saints, you that have engaged in a covenant with him on sacrifices. Shamayim will declare his righteousness, for God is the judge.

Separate the psalm.

Hear, my people, and I will speak to you, Israel, and I will testify to you. I am God, your God.

I will not reprove you on account of your sacrifices, for your whole burnt offerings are before me continually. I will take no bull out of your house, nor he-goats out of your flocks. For all the wild beasts of the thicket are mine, the livestock on the mountains, and oxen. I know all the birds of the sky, and the beauty of the field is mine.

If I should be hungry, I will not tell you, for the world is mine and the fullness of it. Will I eat the flesh of bulls, or drink the blood of goats? Offer to God the sacrifice of praise, and pay your vows to the Highest. Call on me, in the day of affliction, and I will deliver you, and you will glorify me.

Separate the psalm.

But to the sinner, God has said, "Why do you declare my ordinances, and take up my covenant in your mouth?"

Whereas you have hated instruction, and have thrown my words behind you. If you saw a thief, you ran along with him, and have thrown in your lot with adulterers. Your mouth has multiplied iniquity, and your tongue has framed deceit.

You sat and spoke against your brother and scandalized your mother's son. These things you did, and I kept silent. You thought wickedly that I should be like you, but I will reprove you, and set your offense before you. Now consider these things, you that forget God, in case he kills you, and there is no deliverer. The sacrifice of praise will glorify me, which is how I will show him the salvation of God.

Psalms: Chapter 49 Notes

1 Codex Vacticanus: theos theôn cyrios (ΘΕΟϹΘΕѠΝ ΚΥΡΙΟϹ). Translation: god gods (or goddesses) lord

- Aleppo Codex: ål ålhym yhůh (**אל אלהים יהוה**). Translation: El (or God) godesses (or gods in Aramaic) Yhůh
- Leningrad Codex: el elohim yehvah (אֵל אֱלֹהִים יְהֹוָה). Translation: El (or God) godesses (or gods in Aramaic) Yehvah
- Targum to Psalms: ĕlāhā yeyā (אֱלָהָא יְיָ). Translation: god Yah

Psalms: Chapter 50

A psalm of David, when Nathan the prophet came to him when he had gone to Beersheba.

Have mercy on me, God, according to your great mercy, and according to the multitude of your compassion blot out my transgression. Wash me thoroughly from my iniquity, and cleanse me from my sin. For I am conscious of my iniquity, and my sin is continually before me. I have only sinned against you and done evil before you, so you might be justified in your sayings and might overcome when you are judged.

For, look, I was conceived in iniquities, and in sin did my mother conceive me. For, look, you love truth, and you have made known to me the secret and hidden things of your wisdom. You will sprinkle me with hyssop, and I will be purified. You will wash me, and I will be made whiter than snow. You will cause me to hear gladness and joy, the afflicted bones will rejoice.

Turn away your face from my sins, and blot out all my iniquities. Create in me a clean heart, God, and renew a correct breath inside me. Don't drive me away from your presence, and don't remove your holy breath from me. Restore to me the joy of your salvation. Establish me with your ruling wind.

Then I will teach transgressors your ways, and impious men will turn to you. Deliver me from bloodguiltiness, God, the god of my salvation, and my tongue will joyfully declare your righteousness. Lord, you will open my lips, and my mouth will declare your praise. For if you desired sacrifice, I would have given it. You will not take pleasure in whole burnt offerings.

Sacrifice to God is a broken spirit, a broken and humiliated heart God will not despise. Do good, Lord, to Zion in your good pleasure, and let the walls of Jerusalem be built. When will you be pleased with a sacrifice of righteousness, wave-offering, and whole burnt sacrifices? When will they offer calves on your altar?

Psalms: Chapter 51

A psalm of governing by David, when Doeg the Edomite came and told Saul, "David has gone to the house of Abimelech."

Why do you, mighty man, boast of iniquity in your deeds? All the day your tongue has devised unrighteousness, like a sharpened razor you have worked deceit. You have loved iniquity more than goodness, unrighteousness better than to speak righteousness.

Separate the psalm.

You have loved all words of destruction and a deceitful tongue. Therefore God may destroy you forever, may he pluck you up and completely remove you from your living, and your root from the land of the living.

Separate the psalm.

The righteous will see, and fear, and will laugh at him, and say, "Look the man who did not make God his help, but trusted in the abundance of his wealth, and strengthened himself in his vanity."

Yet I am like a fruitful olive in the house of God. I have trusted in the mercy of God forever, even forever. I will give thanks to you forever, for you have done it, and I will wait on your name, for it is good before the saints.

Psalms: Chapter 52

A psalm of instruction of David on Mahalath.

The fool has said in his heart, "There is no God."

They have corrupted themselves, and become abominable in iniquities, and none do good. God looked down from the sky on the sons of Adam, to see if there were any who understood or searched for God. They have all left the way and have altogether become unprofitable. None did good, there was not even one.

Will none of the workers of iniquity know, who devour my people as they would eat bread? They have not called on God. They were greatly afraid, whereas there was no fear for God has scattered the bones of the men-pleasers. They were ashamed, for God despised them. Who will bring the salvation of Israel out of Zion? When the Lord returns those captives from his people, Jacob will celebrate, and Israel will be glad.

Psalms: Chapter 53

For the end, among hymns of instruction by David, when the Ziphites came and said to Saul, "Look, is David not hidden with us?"

Save me, God, by your name, and judge me by your might. God, hear my prayer. Listen to the words of my mouth. For strangers have risen against me, and mighty men have wanted my life. They have not set God before them.

Separate the psalm.

For look! God assists me, and the Lord is the helper of my mind. He will return evil to my enemies, annihilate them in your truth. I will willingly sacrifice to you. I will give thanks to your name, Lord, for it is good. For you have delivered me out of all affliction, and my eye has seen my desire on my enemies.

Psalms: Chapter 54

For the end, among hymns of instruction by David.

Listen, God, to my prayer, and don't ignore my supplication. Attend to me, and listen to me. I was grieved in my meditation, and troubled, because of the voice of the enemy, and because of the oppression of the sinner, for they brought iniquity against me, and were wrathfully angry with me. My heart was troubled within me, and the fear of death fell on me. Fear and trembling came on me, and darkness covered me. I said, "If only I had wings like those of a dove! Then I would flee away, and be at peace."

Look! I have fled far away and lodged in the wilderness.

Separate the psalm.

I waited for he who would deliver me from the distress of spirit and tempest. Destroy, Lord, and divide their tongues, for I have seen iniquity and gainsaying in the city. Day and night it will go around it on its walls, iniquity and sorrow and unrighteousness are in the middle of it, and interest and deceit have not failed from its streets. For if an enemy had insulted me, I would have endured it, and if one who hated me had spoken tauntingly against me, I would have hidden from him. But you, like-minded man, my guide, and my acquaintance, who in companionship with me sweetened our food, and we walked in the temple of God in agreement.

Let death come on them, and let them go down alive into Sheol, for iniquity is in their dwellings, in the middle of them. I cried to God, and the Lord listened to me. Evening, and morning, and at noon I will declare and make known my needs, and he will hear my voice. He will deliver my mind in peace from those who draw near to me, for they were with me in many cases. God will hear, and bring them low, even he that has existed from eternity.

Separate the psalm.

For they have nothing to give in exchange, and therefore they have not feared God. He has reached out his hand for retribution, and they have profaned his covenant. They were scattered at the anger of his countenance, and his heart drew near them. His words were smoother than oil, yet they are arrows. Place your care in the Lord, and he will nourish you, and he will never allow the righteous to be moved. But you, God, will bring them down to the pit of corruption, bloody and cunning men will not live out half their days. I will trust in you, Lord!

Psalms: Chapter 55

For the end, concerning the people that were removed from the sanctuary. By David for a memorial, when the nations caught him in Gath.

Have mercy on me, God, for men have trodden me down and all day long this war has afflicted me. My enemies have trodden me down all day from the dawning of the day, for there are many warring against me. They will be afraid, but I will trust in you.

I will praise God. All day, I have trusted in God, and I will not fear what flesh will do to me. All day long they have hated my words, and all their plans against me are evil. They will live nearby and hide, and they will watch my steps, as I have waited patiently in my mind.

You will on no account save them, and you will bring down the people in anger. God, I have dedicated my life to you, and you have set my tears before you, even according to your promise. My enemies will be turned back, in the day in which I will call on you, look, I know that you are my God.

To God, I will praise his word, and in the Lord will I praise his saying. I have trusted in God, and I will not be afraid of what man will do to me. The vows of your praise, God, which I will pay, are on me. For you have delivered my mind from death, and my feet from slipping so that I should be well-pleasing before God in the land of the living.

Psalms: Chapter 56

For the end. (Don't destroy.) By David. A memorial for when he fled from the presence of Saul to the cave.

Have mercy, on me, God. Have mercy on me, for my mind has trusted in you, and in the shadow of your wings I will trust until iniquity has passed away. I will cry to the Highest God, the God who has benefited me.

Separate the psalm.

He sent from the sky and saved me. He gave it as an insult to those who trampled on me. God has sent forth his mercy and his truth, and he has delivered my mind from the middle of lions' cubs. I lay down to sleep, though troubled. As for the sons of Adam, their teeth were arms and missile weapons, and their tongues were as sharp as swords. Be praised, god above Shamayim, and your glory above all the earth. They have prepared snares for my feet, and have bowed down my mind, and they have dug a pit before my face, and fallen into it themselves.

Separate the psalm.

My heart is ready God, my heart is ready. I will sing, yes I will sing psalms. Awake, my glory. Awake, lute and harp, and I will awake early. Lord, I will give thanks to you among the nations, and I will sing to you among the nations, for your mercy has been praised even to the sky, and your truth to the clouds. Be praised, god above Shamayim, and your glory above all the earth.

Psalms: Chapter 57

For the end. (Don't destroy.) By David. As a memorial.

If you do indeed speak righteousness, then you judge rightly you sons of Adam. For you work iniquities in your hearts in the earth, and your hands plot unrighteousness. Sinners have gone astray from the womb. They go astray from the belly, and they speak lies. Their venom is like that of a serpent, like that of a deaf asp, and that stops her ears, which will not hear the voice of charmers, or follow the poison prepared skillfully by the wise. God has crushed their teeth in their mouth, and God has broken the cheek teeth of the lions. They will completely pass away like water running through, and he will bend his bow until they fail.

They will be destroyed like melted wax, and the fire has fallen and they have not seen the sun. Before your thorns feel the whitethorn, and he will swallow you up alive in his anger. The righteous will rejoice when he sees the vengeance of the impious, and he will wash his hands in the blood of the sinner. A man will say, "Truly then there is fruit for the righteous. Truly there is a God that judges them on the earth."

Psalms: Chapter 58

For the end. (Don't destroy.) By David. As a memorial when Saul sent men and watched his house to kill him.

Deliver me from my enemies, God, and ransom me from those who rise up against me. Deliver me from the workers of iniquity, and save me from bloody men. For, look, they have hunted after my mind, violent men have set on me. Neither is it my iniquity, nor my sin, Lord. Without iniquity, I ran and directed my course right, and awake to help me, and look. You, Lord the god, Sabaoth the god,[1] draw near and visit all the foreigners, and don't pity any who work iniquity.

Separate the psalm.

They will return in the evening, and hunger like a dog, and go around the city. Look, they will speak a voice with their mouth, and a sword is in their lips, for "who," they ask, "has heard?"

But you, Lord, will laugh at them as an insult, and you will completely set at nothing all the foreigners. I will keep my strength looking to you, for you, God, are my helper. As for my God, his mercy will go before me, my god will show me vengeance on my enemies. Don't murder them in case they forget your law, and scatter them through your power, and bring them down, Lord, my defender.

For the sin of their mouth, and the word of their lips, let them be even taken in their pride. For their cursing and falsehood will speak destruction be denounced. They will fall by the anger of speak destruction, and will not be, so they will know that the god of Jacob to lord of the edges of the earth.

Separate the psalm.

They will return in the evening, be hungry like a dog, and go around the city. They will be scattered here and there for meat, and if they are not satisfied, they will murmur. But I will sing to your strength, and in the morning will I celebrate in your mercy for you have been my supporter and my refuge in the day of my affliction. You are my helper, and to you, my God, will I sing. You are my supporter, my god, and my mercy.

Psalms: Chapter 58 Notes

1 Codex Vacticanus: cyrie o theos tôn dynameôn o theos (ΚΥΡΙΕ Ο ΘΕΟϹ ΤΩΝ ΔΥΝΑΜΕΩΝ Ο ΘΕΟϹ). Translation: lord the god of forces the god

• Septuagint manuscript 1219: cyrie tôn dynameôn o theos (ΚΥΡΙΕ ΤΩΝ ΔΥΝΑΜΕΩΝ Ο ΘΕΟϹ). Translation: lord of forces the god

- Dead Sea Scroll 11QPs^d: -ålhy yš- (-אלהי ישר-). Translation: -god Isr-. Only part of the name survives, however, it does appear to match the text in the Aleppo Codex.

- Aleppo Codex: yhůh-ålhym ṣbåůt ålhy yšrål (יהוה-אלהים צבאות אלהי ישראל). Translation: Yhůh-goddesses (or gods in Aramaic, God in Neo-Assyrian) armies gods Israel

- Leningrad Codex: yehvah-elohim | tzeva'ovt elohei yisra'el (יְהוָה־אֱלֹהִים ׀ צְבָאוֹת אֱלֹהֵי יִשְׂרָאֵל). Translation: Yahweh-goddeses (or gods in Aramaic, God in Neo-Assyrian). Armies (or Desires in Aramaic) gods Israel

- Targum to Psalms: yeyā ĕlōhîm ṣebāôt ĕlāhā deyiśrāēl (יְיָ אֱלֹהִים צְבָאוֹת אֱלָהָא דְּיִשְׂרָאֵל). Translation: Yah gods deires god of Israel

The differences between the Greek and Hebrew are notable for not including a reference to Israel. This may be the work of an early Christian redactor but is more likely something that was already in the Aramaic source texts. Psalms has more implied references to Sabaoth and was reportedly sung by the rebels of the Maccabean Revolt, suggesting that the Sabaoth worshipers of the Hellenic era edited this text. By the era, there was a significant division between the Judeans and Samaritans, who called themselves Israelites.

Psalms: Chapter 59

For the end, for those who will yet be changed. For an inscription by David for instruction, when he had burnt Mesopotamia of Syria, Syrian Soba, and returned Joab and slaughtered twelve thousand in the valley of salt.

God, you have rejected and destroyed us, you have been angry, yet have pitied us. You have shaken the earth and troubled it. Heal its breaches, for it has been shaken. You have shown your people hard things. You have made us drink the wine of astonishment. You have given a token to those who fear you, that they might flee from the bow.

Separate the psalm.

So your beloved ones may be delivered, and save with your right hand, and hear me. God has spoken through his sanctified,[1] and I will rejoice, and divide Shechem, and measure out the valley of tents. Gilead is mine, and Manasseh is mine, and Ephraim is the strength of my head. Judah is my king. Moab is the cauldron of my hope. Over Edom will I stretch out my shoe, and the nations have been subjected to me.

Who will lead me into the fortified city? Who will guide me as far as Edom? Will not you, God, who has thrown us away? Will not you, God, go out with our forces? Give us help from trouble, for vain is the deliverance of man. In God will we work great power, and he will bring to nothing those who harass us.

Psalms: Chapter 59 Notes

1 Codex Vacticanus: tô agiô autou (ΤѠΛΓΙѠΑΥΤΟΥ). Translation: the saint (or holiness) of him

- Aleppo Codex: bqdšŭ (בקדשו). Translation: with his sanctified

- Leningrad Codex: bekadeshov (בְּקָדְשׁוֹ). Translation: with his sanctified

Psalms: Chapter 60

For the end. Among the Hymns of David.

God, listen to my petition and listen to my prayer. From the edges of the earth have I cried to you, when my heart was in trouble, and you lifted me up on a rock you did guide me because you were my hope, a tower of strength from the face of the enemy. I will live in your tabernacle forever, and I will shelter myself under the shadow of your wings.

Separate the psalm.

For you, God, have heard my prayers, and you have given an inheritance to those who fear your name. You will add days to the days of the king, and you will lengthen his years to all generations. He will endure forever before God, and which of them will seek out his mercy and truth? So I will sing to your name forever and ever, that I may daily perform my vows.

Psalms: Chapter 61

A psalm of David for Idithun.

Won't my mind be subjected to God? For he is my salvation. For he is my god, and my savior, and my helper, I will not be moved anymore. How long will you assault a man? You are all slaughtering as with a bowed wall and a broken hedge. They only took counsel to set at nothing my honor, and I ran in thirst. With their mouth they blessed, but with their heart they cursed.

Separate the psalm.

Nevertheless, my mind, be subjected to God. For he is my patient hope. For he is my God and my savior and my helper, I will not be moved. God is my salvation and my glory. He is the God of my help, and my trust is in God. Trust in him, all you congregation of the people. Pour out your hearts before him, for God is our helper.

Separate the psalm.

But the sons of Adam are vain, and the sons of Adam are false, to be deceitful in the balances. They are altogether formed out of vanity. Don't trust in unrighteousness, and don't lust after robberies. If wealth should flow in, don't set your heart on it. God has spoken once, and I have heard these two things, that power is of God, and mercy is yours, Lord, for you will reward everyone according to his works.

Psalms: Chapter 62

A psalm of David, when he was in the wilderness of Edom.

God, my god, I cry to you early, and my mind has thirsted for you. How often has my flesh longed after you, in a barren and trackless desert! Thus have I appeared before you in the sanctuary, that I might see your power and your glory. For your mercy is better than lives, and my lips will praise you. Thus I will bless you during my life. I will lift up my hands in your name. Let my mind be filled as if with marrow and fatness, and my joyful lips will praise your name.

Since I have remembered you on my bed, and in the early seasons, I have meditated on you. For you have been my helper, and in the shelter of your wings will I rejoice. My mind has been glued very close behind you, and your right hand has upheld me. But they vainly wanted after my mind, and they will go into the lowest parts of the earth. They will be delivered up to the power of the sword, and they will be portions for foxes. But the king will rejoice in God, and everyone who swears by him will be praised, and for the mouth of those who speak unjust things has been stopped.

Psalms: Chapter 63

A psalm of David.

Hear my prayer, God, when I make my petition to you, and deliver my mind from the fear of the enemy. You have sheltered me from the conspiracy of those who do wickedly, and from the multitude of those who work iniquity, and who have sharpened their tongues like a sword. They have bent their bow maliciously to shoot in secret at the blameless, and they will shoot him suddenly, and will not fear.

They have set up for themselves an evil matter, they have given counsel to hide snares, and they have said, "Who will see them?"

They have searched out iniquity, and they have wearied themselves with searching diligently, a man will approach and the heart is deep, and God will be praised, their wounds were caused by the weapon of the foolish children, and their tongues have set him at nothing. All who saw them were troubled, and every man was alarmed, and they related the works of God and understood his deeds. The righteous will rejoice in the Lord, and trust in him, and all the upright in heart will be praised.

Psalms: Chapter 64

A Psalm and Song of David.

Praise becomes you, god in Zion, and to you will the vow be performed. Hear my prayer, and to you, all flesh will come. The words of transgressors have overpowered us, but you pardon our sins. Blessed is he who you have chosen and adopted, and he will live in your courts. We will be filled with the good things of your house, and your temple is holy.

You are wonderful in righteousness. Listen to us, God our savior, the hope of all the edges of the earth, and of those who are on the sea far away. You who prepare the mountains in your strength, being girded about with power, you who trouble the depth of the sea, the sounds of its waves.

The nations will be troubled, and those who inhabit the edges of the earth will be afraid of your signs, and you will cause the exits of morning and evening to rejoice. You have visited the earth and saturated it, and you have abundantly enriched it. The river of God is filled with water, and you have prepared their food, for this is the preparation of it. Saturate her furrows, multiply her fruits, and the crop springing up will rejoice in its drops.

You will bless the crown of the year because of your goodness, and your plains will be filled with oil. The mountains of the wilderness will be enriched, and the hills will gird themselves with joy. The rams of the flock are clothed with wool, and the valleys will abound in grain, and they will cry aloud, yes they will sing hymns.

Psalms: Chapter 65

For the end, a song of the psalm of resurrection.

Shout to God, all the earth. Sing praises to his name, and give glory to his praise. Say to God, "How amazing are your works!"

Through the greatness of your power, your enemies will lie to you. Let all the earth worship you, and sing to you, let them sing to your name.

Separate the psalm.

Come and look at the works of God, and he is terrible in his counsels beyond the children of men. Who turns the sea into desert, and they will go through the river on foot. There we will rejoice in him, who by his power has dominion forever, his eyes look on the nations. Don't let those who provoke him, be praised themselves.

Separate the psalm.

Bless our God, you nations, and make the voice of his praise to be heard, who quickens my mind in life, and does not allow my feet to be moved. For you, God has tested us, you have tested us with fire as silver is tested. You brought us into the snare, and you laid plagues on our backs.

You did mount men on our heads, and we went through the fire and water, but you brought us out into a place of refreshment. I will go into your temple with whole burnt offerings, and I will pay my vows, which my lips framed, and my mouth spoke in my affliction. I will offer to you whole burnt sacrifices full of marrow, with incense and rams, and I will sacrifice to you oxen with goats.

Separate the psalm.

Come, hear, and I will tell, all you that fear God, what great things he has done for my mind. I cried to him with my mouth and praised him with my tongue. If I have regarded iniquity in my heart, don't let the Lord listen to me. Therefore God has listened to me, he has attended to the voice of my prayer. Blessed be God, who has not turned away my prayer, nor his mercy from me.

Psalms: Chapter 66

A psalm of David among the Hymns.

God be merciful to us and bless us, and cause his face to shine on us.

Separate the psalm.

So men may know your way on the earth, your salvation among all nations, let the nations, God, give thanks to you, and let all the nations give thanks to you. Let the nations rejoice and celebrate, for you will judge the peoples in equity, and will guide the nations on the earth.

Separate the psalm.

Let the people, God, give thanks to you, and let all the people give thanks to you. The earth has yielded her fruit, and let God, our god bless us. Let God bless us, and let all the edges of the earth fear him.

Psalms: Chapter 67

A psalm of a song by David.

Let God arise, and let his enemies be scattered, and let those who hate him flee from before him. As smoke vanishes, let them vanish, as wax melts before the fire, so let the sinners perish from before God. But let the righteous rejoice, and let them celebrate before God, let them be delighted with joy. Sing to God, sing praises to his name, and make a way for he who goes to the sunsets.[1] Lord is his name, and celebrate before him. They will be troubled before the face of him, who is the father of the orphans, and judge of the widows. Such is God in his holy place.

God settles the solitary in a house and leads out many prisoners, also those who act provokingly, even those who live in tombs. God, when you went out before your people when you went through the wilderness.

Separate the psalm.

The earth quaked. Yes, the sky dropped water in the presence of the god of Sinai, at the presence of the god in Israel. God, you will grant to your inheritance a gracious rain, for it was weary, but you refreshed it. Your creatures live in it, and you have in your goodness prepared for the poor. The Lord gives a word to those who preach in a great company. The king of the forces of the beloved, of the beloved, even for the beauty of the house to divide the spoils.

Even if you should lie among the lots, you will have the wings of a dove covered with silver and her breast with yellow gold. When the heavenly one scatters kings on it, they will be made snow-white in Zalmon. The mountain of God is a rich mountain, a mountain curdled like cheese, a rich mountain. Therefore do you conceive evil, you mountains curdled like cheese? This is the mountain which God has delighted to live in, yes, the Lord will live in it forever. The chariots of God are ten thousand, thousands of rejoicing ones. The Lord is among them, in Sinai, in the holy place. You have gone up on high, you have led captivity captive, you have received gifts for man, yes, for they were rebellious, that you might live among them. Blessed is the Lord the god, blessed is the Lord daily, and the God of our salvation will bless us.

Separate the psalm.

Our god is the god of salvation, and to the Lord belong the issues from death. But God will crush the heads of his enemies, the hairy crown of those who go on in their trespasses.

The Lord said, "I will bring again from Bashan, I will bring my people again through the depths of the sea.

That your foot may be dipped in blood, and the tongue of your dogs be stained with that of your enemies."

Your business, God has seen, and the business of my god, the king, in the sanctuary. The princes went first, next before the players on instruments, in the middle of damsels playing on timbrels. Praise God in the congregations, the Lord from the fountains of Israel. There is Benjamin the younger one in ecstasy, the princes of Judah their rulers, the princes of Zebulun, the princes of Naphtali. God, command you your strength. Strengthen, God, this which you have worked in us. Because of your temple at Jerusalem will kings bring presents to you.

Rebuke the wild beasts of the reed, and let the crowd of bulls with the heifers of the nations be rebuked, so that they who have been proved with silver may not be shut out. Scatter the nations that wish for wars. Ambassadors will arrive out of Egypt. Kush[2] will hurry to stretch out her hand readily to God. Sing to God, you kingdoms of the earth. Sing psalms to the Lord.

Separate the psalm.

Sing to God that climbs into the sky above Shamayim in the east. Look, he will speak a mighty sound with his voice. Give glory to God, his excellency is over Israel, and his power is in the clouds. God is wonderful among his holy ones, the god in Israel will give power and strength to his people. Blessed be God.

Psalms: Chapter 67 Notes

1 Codex Vacticanus: epi dysmôn (ἐπὶ δυσμων). Translation: to the sunsets (west)

• Aleppo Codex: bôrbŭt (בערבות). Translation: on plains (or deserts)

• Leningrad Codex: ba'aravovt (בָּעֲרָבֹ֑ות). Translation: on plains (or deserts)

• Vetus Latina manuscripts: super caelos caelorum. Translation: above (or over, upwards) skies (or vaulted skies) of skies

• Targum to Psalms: baărābôt (בַּעֲרָבֹות). Translation: on steppes (or deserts)

2 Codex Vacticanus: Aethiopia (αιθιοπια). Translation: Sudan (or Kush)

• Aleppo Codex: kŭš (כוש). Translation: Kush (or Sudan)

• Leningrad Codex: kush (כּוּשׁ). Translation: Kush (or Sudan)

• Targum to Psalms: kûš (כוּשׁ). Translation: Kush (or Sudan)

Kush was an ancient civilization in modern Sudan, which the Greeks later called Aethiopia. Due to the confusion from the similarity named Ethiopia, which is farther southeast, the term Kush is imported from the Masoretic texts.

Psalms: Chapter 68

A psalm of David, for alternate strains.

Save me, God, for the waters have come into my mind. I am stuck fast in a deep mire, and there is no standing. I have come into the depths of the sea, and a storm has overwhelmed me. I am weary of crying, my throat has become hoarse, and my eyes have failed by my waiting on my God.

They who hate me without cause are more than the hairs of my head. The enemies that persecute me unrighteously are strengthened. Then I paid for that which I did not take away. God, you know my foolishness, and my transgressions are not hidden from you. Don't let those who wait on you Lord, my Lord Sabaoth,[1] be ashamed on my account. Don't let those who seek you, be ashamed on my account, god in Israel. I have allowed insult for your sake, and shame has covered my face. I became strange to my brothers, and a stranger to my mother's children. For the zeal of your house has eaten me up, and the insults of those who insulted you have fallen on me. I bowed down my mind with fasting, and that was made my reproach. I put on sackcloth for my covering, and I became a proverb to them. They who sit in the gate talked against me, and those who drank wine sang against me.

But I will cry to you, Lord, in my prayer, God, it is a propitious time. In the multitude of your mercy hear me, in the truth of your salvation. Save me from the mire, so I don't become stuck in it, and let me be saved from those who hate me, and from the deep waters. Don't let the floodwater drown me, nor let the deep swallow me up, nor let the well shut its mouth to me. Hear me, Lord, for your mercy is good, according to the multitude of your compassion look on me. Don't turn away from your servant, for I am afflicted, hear me quickly.

Come close to my mind and redeem it. Deliver me because of my enemies. For you know my reproach, and my shame, and my confusion, all that afflict me are before you. My mind has waited for reproach and misery. I waited for one to grieve with me, but there was none, and for one to comfort me, but I found none. They also gave me gall for my food and made me drink vinegar for my thirst. Let their table be a snare before them, repayment, and a stumbling block. Let their eyes be darkened that they should not see, and bow down their back continually. Pour out your anger on them, and let the fury of your anger take hold of them. Let their homes be made desolate, and let there be no inhabitant in their tents. Because they persecuted him whom you have struck, and they have added to the grief of my wounds.

Add iniquity to their iniquity, and let them not come into your righteousness. Let them be blotted out of the book of the living, and let them not be written with the righteous. I am poor and sad, but the salvation of your countenance has helped me. I will praise the name of my God with a song, I will magnify him with praise, and this will please God more than a young calf having horns and hoofs.

Let the poor see and rejoice, and seek the Lord diligently, and you will live. The Lord hears the poor and does not ignore his fettered ones. Praise him Shamayim and Eretz, Yam[2] and everything moving in him, and all things moving on the Earth. For God will save Zion, and the cities of Judah will be built, and men will live there and inherit it. The descendants of his servants will possess it, and those who love his name will live there.

Psalms: Chapter 68 Notes

1 Codex Vacticanus: cyrie cyrie tôn dynameôn (ΚΥΡΙΕ ΚΥΡΙΕΤΩΝΔΥΝΑΜΕΩΝ). Translation: lord lord of forces
• Codex Sinaiticus: cyrie tôn dynameôn (ΚΥΡΙΕΤΩΝ ΔΥΝΑΜΕΩΝ). Translation: lord of forces

• Dead Sea Scroll 4QPsᵃ: å--ůh- (- תו--א). The section of text is very damaged but does indicate that ådny yhůh was likely present.

• Aleppo Codex: ådny yhůh sbåůt (**אדני יהוה צבאות**).
Translation: my lord Yahweh of armies

• Leningrad Codex: adonai yehvih tzeva'ovt (אֲדֹנָי יְהוִה
צְבָאוֹת). Translation: my lord Yehvih of armies

2 Codex Vacticanus: ouranoe cae ê gê thalassa (ΟΥΡΑΝΟΙ
ΚΑΙΗΓΗΘΑΛΑϹϹΑ). Translation: skies and earth, sea

• Aleppo Codex: šmm ůårs ymm (**שמים וארץ ימים**).
Translation: skies and land seas

• Leningrad Codex: shamayim va'aretz yammim (שָׁמַיִם
וָאָרֶץ יַמִּים). Translation: Shamayim (or skies) and Eretz (or Earth) seas

• Targum to Psalms: yamayā (יַמְיָא). Translation: sea

214

Psalms: Chapter 69

By David for a remembrance. So the Lord may save me.

Come close, God, to assist me. Let them be ashamed and confused who seek my mind. Let those be turned backward and put to shame, who wish me evil. Let those who say to me, "Hear, hear," only be turned back and put to shame immediately.

Let all who seek you celebrate and be glad in you, and let those who love your salvation say continually, "Let God be praised."

I am poor and needy, God, help me. You are my helper and deliverer, Lord, don't delay.

Psalms: Chapter 70

By David. A Psalm sung by the sons of Jehonadab, and the first that were taken captive.

Lord, I have trusted in you, let me never be put to shame. In your righteousness deliver me and rescue me, and turn your ear to me, and save me. Be for me a protecting god, and a stronghold to save me, for you are my fortress and my refuge. Deliver me, my god, from the hand of the sinner, from the hand of the transgressor and unjust man. For you are my support, Lord. Lord, you were my hope from my youth.

On you have I been stayed from the womb, from the belly of my mother you are my protector, to you is my singing continually. I have become as it were a wonder to many, but you are my strong helper. Let my mouth be filled with praise, that I may hymn your glory, and your majesty all day.

Don't throw me away at the time of old age. Don't forget me when my strength fails. For my enemies have spoken against me, and those who lay wait for my mind have taken counsel together, saying, "God has forgotten him. Persecute and trap him, as there is no one to deliver him."

God, don't go far from me, my god, come close and be my help. Let those who plot against my mind be ashamed and completely fail. Let those who seek my hurt be clothed with shame and dishonor. But I will hope continually and will praise you more and more. My mouth will declare your righteousness openly, and your salvation all the day, for I am not acquainted with the affairs of men. I will go on in the might of the Lord. Lord, I will make mention of your righteousness only.

God, you have taught me from my youth, and from now I will declare your wonders, even until I am old and advanced in years. God, don't forget me until I have declared your strength to all the generations that are to come, even your power and your righteousness, God, up to the highest sky, even the mighty works which you have done. God, who is like to you?

What plagues and many sore have you shown me! Yet you turned and quickened me, and brought me again from the depths of the earth. You did multiply your righteousness, and did turn and comfort me, and brought me again out of the depths of the earth. I will also, therefore, give thanks to you, God, because of your truth, on an instrument of melody I will sing psalms to you on the harp, Holy One of Israel. My lips will rejoice when I sing to you, and my mind, which you have redeemed. Moreover, also my tongue will meditate all day on your righteousness, and when they are ashamed and confused who seek to hurt me.

Psalms: Chapter 71

For Solomon.

God, give your judgment to the king, and your right-eousness to the king's son, that he may judge your people with righteousness, and your poor with judgment. Let the mountains and the hills raise peace to your people, and he will judge the poor of the people in righteousness, and save the children of the needy, and will bring low the false accuser. He will continue as long as the sun and before the moon forever. He will come down like rain on a fleece, and as drops falling on the earth.

In his days will righteousness spring up, and abundance of peace until the moon is removed. He will have dominion from sea to sea, and from the river to the edges of the earth. The Kushite will fall before him, and his enemies will lick the dust.

The kings of Tharsis and the Isles, will bring presents, and the kings of the Arabians and Saba[1] will offer gifts. All kings will worship him, and all the nations will serve him for he has delivered the poor from the oppressor, and the needy who had no helper. He will spare the poor and needy and will deliver the minds of the needy. He will redeem their minds from interest and injustice, and their name will be precious before him. He will live, and the gold of Arabia will be given to him, and men will pray for him continually, and all day they will praise him.

There will be an establishment on the earth on the tops of the mountains, and the fruit will be praised above Lebanon, and they of the city will flourish like the grass of the earth. Let his name be blessed forever, and his name will endure as long as the sun,[2] and all the tribes of the earth will be blessed in him, and all nations will call him blessed. Blessed is Lord the god, the god of Israel, who alone does wonders. Blessed is his glorious name forever, even forever and ever, and all the earth will be filled with his glory. So be it, so be it.

The hymns of David the son of Jesse have ended.

Psalms: Chapter 71 Notes

1 Codex Vacticanus: Saba (ⲤⲁⲂⲁ)
• Aleppo Codex: šbå (שְׁבָא)
• Leningrad Codex: sheva (שְׁבָא)
• Targum to Psalms: šebā (שְׁבָא)

Saba was a country in the territory of modern Yemen between 1200 BC and 275 AD. This nation is also mentioned in the Septuagint's books of 3rd Kingdoms, Job, Joel, Ezekiel, and Isaiah, as well as the Quran's An-Naml and Saba surahs. This country was ultimately conquered by the neighboring Himyarite Kingdom around 275 AD, which was itself then conquered by the Ethiopian Axumite Empire around 525 AD. The Himyarite Kingdom was an officially Jewish State after 390 AD and is likely the origin of the early Arabic language version of the Kebra Nagast, which was later translated into Ge'ez, and Ethiopianized, making the "Queen of Saba" a monarch from the Ethiopian Highlands. The Kebra Nagast has never been used by the Beta Israel community in Ethiopia, who consider it a later Christian work.

2 Codex Vacticanus: tou hêliou (ΤΟΥΗΛΙΟΥ). Translation: the sun

- Aleppo Codex: šmš (שמש). Translation: Shamesh (or sun)
- Leningrad Codex: Shemesh (שֶׁמֶשׁ). Translation: Shamesh (or sun)
- Targum to Psalms: šemêh (שְׁמֵיה). Translation: sky

Psalms: Chapter 72

A Psalm for Asaph.

How good is God to Israel, to the upright in heart! But my feet were almost overthrown, and my steps very nearly slipped. For I was jealous of the transgressors, seeing the tranquility of sinners. For there is no sign of reluctance in their death, and they have firmness under their affliction. They are not in the troubles of other men, and they will not be scourged with other men. Therefore pride has possessed them, they have clothed themselves with their injustice and impiousness. Their injustice will go out like oil, and they have fulfilled their intention.

They have taken counsel and spoken in iniquity, they have said unrighteousness loftily. They have set their mouth against Shamayim, and their tongue has gone through on the earth. Therefore will my people return here, and full days will be found in them. They said, "How does God know?" and "Is there knowledge in the Highest?"

Look, these are the sinners, and those who prosper always, have possessed wealth. I said, "Truly in vain have I justified my heart, and washed my hands in innocence."

I was plagued all day, and my reproof was every morning. If I said, "I will speak thus, look, I should have broken covenant with the generation of your children."

I undertook to understand this, but it is too hard for me until I go into the sanctuary of God, and so understand the latter end. Certainly, you have appointed judgments to them because of their cunning dealings, you have thrown them down when they were lifted. How they have become desolate! Suddenly, they have failed, and they have perished because of their iniquity. As the dream of one awakening, Lord, in your city, you will despise their image.

My heart has rejoiced, and my reins have been changed. But I was vile and did not know. I became brutish before you. Yet I am continually with you. You have held my right hand. You have guided me by your counsel, and you have taken me to yourself with glory. For what have I in the sky but you? What have I desired on the earth beside you? My heart and my flesh have failed. God is the strength of my heart, and God is my portion forever. For, look, those who remove themselves far from you will perish. You have destroyed everyone that goes a whoring from you. But it is good for me to cling close to God, to put my trust in the Lord, that I may proclaim all your praises in the gates of the daughter of Zion.

Psalms: Chapter 73

A psalm of understanding for Asaph.

Why have you rejected us, God, forever? Why is your anger started against the sheep of your pasture? Remember your congregation which you have purchased from the beginning, and you ransomed the land of your inheritance, Mount Zion in which you have lived. Lift your hands against their pride continually, and because of all that, the enemy has done wickedly in your holy places. They that hate you have boasted in the middle of your feast, and they have set up their standards for signs, ignorantly as it were in the entrance above, they cut down its doors at once with axes as in a wood of trees, and they have broken it down with hatchet and stone cutter.

They have burnt your sanctuary with fire to the ground, and they have profaned the tabernacle of your name. They have said in their heart, even all their families together, come, let us abolish the feasts of the Lord from the earth. We have not seen our signs, and there is no longer a prophet, and God will not know us anymore. How long, God, will the enemy insult? Will the enemy provoke your name forever? Will you turn away your hand, and your right hand from the middle of your chest forever? But God is our king before the age, and he has worked salvation on the earth.

You established the sea through your might, you broke to pieces the heads of the dragon in the rainwater.[1] You broke to pieces the heads of Leviathan[2] and you gave him as meat to the Kushites.[3] You clogged fountains and torrents, and you dried up mighty rivers. The day is yours, and the night is yours. You have prepared the sun and the moon. You have made all the edges of the earth, and you have made summer and spring. Remember your creation, an enemy has insulted the Lord, and a foolish people have provoked your name.

Don't deliver to the wild beasts a mind that praises to you. Don't forget forever the minds of your poor. Look on your covenant, for the dark places of the earth are filled with the habitations of iniquity. Don't let the afflicted and shamed one be rejected, and the poor and needy will praise your name. Rise, God, plead your cause, and remember the insults that come from the foolish one all day. Don't forget the voice of your supplicants, and let the pride of those who hate you continually ascend before you.

Psalms: Chapter 73 Notes

1 Codex Vacticanus: dracontôn epi tou ydatos (ΔΡΑΚΟΝΤΩΝ ΕΠΙ ΤΟΥ ΥΔΑΤΟC). Translation: dragon in the rainwater

- Aleppo Codex: tnynym ôl-hmym (‏תנינים על־המים‎).
Translation: crocodile in the waters
- Leningrad Codex: tanninim al-hammayim (‏תַּנִּינִים‎
‏עַל־הַמָּיִם‎). Translation: crocodile in the waters
- Vetus Latina manuscripts: draco in super aquam.
Translation: dragon in upper water
- Targum to Psalms: miṣrāê al yamā (‏מִצְרָאֵי עַל יַמָא‎).
Translation: Egyptians upon sea

The sources all agree that it is fresh water and not sea water however, the Greek and Latin texts indicate it is the upper waters, above the sky. The Hebrew terms match the words used in Bereshit chapter 1, where the "great crocodile" (‏תַּנִּינִם‎ ‏הַגְּדֹלִים‎) was created in the "fresh waters" (‏הַמַּיִם‎) alongside all flying creatures, suggesting this is the same "sky crocodile." The Greeks translated the terms in Cosmic Genesis Great Cetus (ΚΗΤΗ ΤΑ ΜΕΓΑΛΑ) of the rainwater (ΥΔΑΤΟΣ), indicating they believed the "sky dragon" was the constellation Cetus. This dragon in Cosmic Genesis was created along with the sun, moon, and stars, suggesting it is the Galactic Great Rift. In ancient Middle Eastern mythology, the dark band that divides the night sky was often interpreted as a great dragon or coiled serpent, which ruled the night the same way the sun ruled the day.

2 Codex Vaticanus: dracontos (ΔΡΑΚΟΝΤΟΣ). Translation: dragon
- Codex Veronensis: dracontos tou megalou (ΔΡΑΚΟΝΤΟΣ ΤΟΥΜΕΓΑΛΟΥ). Translation: dragon the great

- Aleppo Codex: lǔytn (לִוית). Translation: Leviathan
- Leningrad Codex: livyatan (לִוְיָתָן). Translation: Leviathan
- Targum to Psalms: gibbārê parōh (גִבְרֵי פַרְעֹה). Translation: strong Pharaoh

Leviathan shows up a few times in the Masoretic text, specifically in the books of Psalms, Job, and Isaiah. Psalms and Job contain some of the oldest verses in the Masoretic texts and are both steeped in Canaanite gods and imagery. The Leviathan is generally accepted as being a later development of the name Lotan (𒈗—➤➤), the coiled sea monster from the Ugaritic texts from northern Canaan which themselves date back to between 1400 and 1300 BC. In the Ugaritic texts, Lotan was one of the servants of Yam (Sea) who fought against Hadad (Ba'al) when Yam tried to usurp the rule of the gods.

In both instances where Leviathan was referenced in Psalms it was translated as "dragon" in Greek, however, the term that is livyatan (לִוְיָתָן) in the Masoretic text, is Cetus the great (ΚΗΤΗ ΤΑ ΜΕΓΑΛΑ), the same term used several other places in the Septuagint, including in Genesis, Psalms, and Job. A similar term, Dragon the Great, was also used in this verse in the Codex Veronensis from the 6th century, suggesting that at least one scribe believed Leviathan was Cetus the Great. Nevertheless, Lotan / Leviathan was a sea creature and not a sky creature. Based on the descriptions in Job, Leviathan was a scaley monster, that was able to leave the sea and walk on land. This reference in Psalms claims he was killed and fed on by the Aethiopians / Kushites. In most respects, the Septuagint's references to the Leviathan match the Cetus monster from the Perseus epic in Greek mythology, which is no doubt why the Greeks chose that name. In the Greek epic, the hero Perseus traveled to Aethiopia, where he killed the Cetus, a large monster that was coming out of the sea and attacking the Aethiopians.

Lotan was described in the Ugaritic texts as being a seven-headed serpent, virtually identical to the seven-headed dragon from the Revelation of John which contains translation errors from older Aramaic texts, suggesting Lotan / Leviathan continued to exist in Aramaic texts until the Christian era. Moreover, the beginning of Isaiah chapter 27 is very similar to a section of the ancient Ugaritic texts, with the name Leviathan replacing Lotan in Isaiah's work. This strongly suggests that at least some parts of the Ugaritic texts were still in circulation by Isaiah's time, and possibly as late as the 1st century of the Christian era. The earliest surviving depiction of the battle between Ba'al Hadad and Lotan has been found on seals in Syria dating back to between the 18th and 16th century BC, however, similar depictions of a multi-headed dragon being slain date to the 3rd millennium BC in ancient Sumer.

3 Codex Vacticanus: laoes toes Aithiopsin (ΛΛΟΙϹΤΟΙϹ ΑΙΘΙΟΤΙΝ). Translation: peoples of Aethopia

• Aleppo Codex: lôm lsyym (לְעַם לְצִיִּים). Translation: the nation of the ships

• Leningrad Codex: le'am letziyyim (לְעַם לְצִיִּים). Translation: the nation of the ships

PSALMS: CHAPTER 73

- Targum to Psalms: gûšemêhôn lîrôdê (גּוּשְׁמֵיהוֹן לִירוֹדֵי).

Translation: alliance from Ionia of Rhodes

The Greek interpretation appears to be a reference to the story of Perseus killing the reptilian sea monster Cetus in Aethiopia from Greek mythology. The Hebrew version verse suggests an older story, related to the Sea Peoples' invasion of Egypt at the end of the New Kingdom era, which shattered Egyptian control of southern Canaan, allowing the Pelesets to take control of the region. Egypt was sometimes called Leviathan in older Israelite texts, partly because of the king's crown, which was shaped like a cobra's head, and partly because the Nile had seven mouths draining into the Mediterranean. It is likely the Greek translators substituted the illusions to Perseus because they believed the "Nation of the ships" sounded like the Greeks. The Targum of Psalms version seems to be a reference to the Alliance of Sea Peoples which attacked Egypt and ultimately led to the collapse of the Egyptian New Kingdom circa 1200 BC.

Psalms: Chapter 74

For the end. (Don't destroy.) A psalm of a Song for Asaph.

We will give thanks to you, God, we will give thanks, and call on your name. I will declare all your wonderful works. When I will take a set time, I will judge righteously. The earth is dissolved, and all who live in it. I have strengthened its pillars.

Separate the psalm.

I said to the transgressors, "Do not transgress," and to the sinners, "Don't lift up the horn."

Don't lift your horn on high, and don't speak unrighteousness against God. For good comes neither from the east, nor from the west, nor the desert mountains. For God is the judge, he puts down one and raises another. For there is a cup in the hand of the Lord, full of unmingled wine, and he has turned it from this into that, but its dregs have not been completely poured out, and all the sinners of the earth will drink them. But I will celebrate forever. I will sing praises to the God of Jacob. I will break all the horns of sinners, but the horns of the righteous one will be praised.

Psalms: Chapter 75

For the end, among the Hymns, a psalm for Asaph, a Song for the Assyrian.

God is known in Judah, and his name is great in Israel. His home has been in Salem,[1] and his home is on Zion. There he broke the power of the bows, the shield, and the sword, and the battle.

Separate the psalm.

You do wonderfully shine forth from the eternal mountains. All the simple ones in the heart were troubled, and all the men of wealth have slept their sleep, and have found nothing in their hands. At your rebuke, God of Jacob, the riders on horses slumbered. You are terrible, and who will withstand you, because of your anger? You did cause judgment to be heard from the sky, and the earth was afraid, and was still when God arose to judgment, to save all the meek in heart.

Separate the psalm.

For the inward thought of man will give thanks to you, and the memorial of his inward thought will keep a feast to you. Vow, and pay your vows to the Lord our god, and all that is around him will bring gifts, even to him that is terrible, and that takes away the spirits of princes, so he that is terrible among the kings of the earth.

Psalms: Chapter 75 Notes

1 Codex Vacticanus: irênê (ЄΙΡΗΝΗ). Translation: peace

- Aleppo Codex: šlm (שׁלם). Translation: Salem (or complete, safe)

- Leningrad Codex: shalem (שָׁלֵם). Translation: Salem (or complete, safe)

Based on the context, it appears the Greek translators translated the name of the city of Salem as "peace," which is what the name means. As it is a geographic reference, the city's name is restored here to Salem. According to Jeremiah, Salem was the name of a city in Samaria, near modern Nabulus.

Psalms: Chapter 76

A psalm of Asaph for Idithun.

I cried to the Lord with my voice, yes, my voice was addressed to God, and he heard me. On the day of my affliction, I earnestly searched for the Lord with my hands at night before him, and I was not deceived. My mind refused to be comforted. I remembered God and rejoiced. I poured out my complaint, and my mind fainted.

Separate the psalm.

All my enemies set a watch against me. I was troubled and did not speak. I considered the days of old and remembered ancient years. I meditated. I communed with my heart by night, and diligently searched my spirit, saying, "Will the Lord throw me away forever? Will he never be pleased? Will he cut off his mercy forever, even for all eternity? Will God forget to pity? Will he shut away his compassion because of his anger?"

Separate the psalm.

I said, "Now I have begun. This is the change of the right hand of the Highest. I remembered the works of the Lord, for I will remember your wonders from the beginning. I will meditate on all your works and will consider your actions. God, your way is in the sanctuary, and who is as great a god as our god? You are the god who does wonders. You have made known your power among the nations. You have with your arm, redeemed your people, the sons of Jacob and Joseph."

Separate the psalm.

The waters saw you, God, the waters saw you and were afraid, and the depths were troubled. There was an abundant sound of water. The clouds spoke a voice, for your arrows went abroad. The voice of your thunder was abroad, and your lightning appeared to the world, and the earth trembled a quaked. Your way is in the sea, and your paths in many waters and your footsteps can't be known. You guided your people like sheep by the hand of Moses and Aaron.

Psalms: Chapter 77

A psalm of understanding for Asaph.

Pay attention, my people, to my law. Incline your ear to the words of my mouth.

I will open my mouth in parables. I will say hidden things that have existed from the beginning.

All of which we have heard and known and our fathers have told to us.

They were not hidden from their children to the second generation. The fathers declaring the praises of the Lord, and his mighty acts, and his wonders which he worked.

He raised up a testimony in Jacob and appointed a law in Israel, which he commanded our fathers, to make it known to their children that another generation might know, the sons which should be born, and they should rise and tell them to their children, so they might set their trust in God, and not forget the works of God, but diligently seek his commandments.

That they should not be like their fathers, a perverse and provoking generation, a generation that did not set its heart right, and its spirit was not faithful to God. The children of Ephraim, bending and shooting with the bow, turned back on the day of battle. They did not keep the covenant of God, and would not follow his law.

They forgot his benefits, and his miracles which he had shown them, the miracles which he worked before their forefathers in the land of Egypt, and in the plain along the way.[1] He divided the sea and led them through, while he made the waters to stand as in a bottle. He guided them with a cloud by day, and all night with the fire-lightning,[2] he divided a rock in the wilderness and made them drink greatly. He brought water out of the rock and caused water to flow down like rivers.

Yet they sinned more against him, and they provoked the Highest in the wilderness. They tempted God in their hearts, in asking meat for the desire of their minds. They spoke against God, and said, "Will God be able to prepare a table in the wilderness? As he struck the rock, and the waters flowed, and the torrents ran abundantly, will he also be able to give bread, or prepare a table for his people?"

Therefore the Lord heard and was provoked, and a fire was started in Jacob, and anger went up against Israel, because they did not believe in God, and did not trust in his salvation. Yet he commanded the clouds from above and opened the doors of the sky, and rained on them manna to eat, and gave them the bread of the sky. Man ate messengers' food, and he sent them enough provisions to fill them. He removed the south wind from the sky, and by his might, he brought in the southwest wind. He rained on them flesh like dust and feathered birds like the sand of the seas. They fell into the middle of their camp, around their tents. So they ate and were filled, and he gave them their desire. They were not disappointed in their desire, but when their food was yet in their mouth, then the indignation of God rose against them, and killed the fattest of them, and overthrew the choice men of Israel.

During this time, they sinned even more and did not believe in his miracles. Their days were consumed in vanity, and their years with anxiety. When he killed them, they searched for him, and they returned and called on God as they had before. They remembered that God was their helper, and the Highest God was their redeemer. Yet they loved him only with their mouth, and lied to him with their tongue, for their heart was not right with him, neither were they steadfast in his covenant.

Yet he is compassionate, and merciful to their sins, and will not destroy them. Yes, he will frequently turn away his anger, and will not kindle all his anger. He remembered that they are flesh, a wind that passes away and does not return. How often did they provoke him in the wilderness, and anger him in the desert?

Yes, they turned back, tempted God, and provoked the Holy One of Israel. They did not remember his hand on the day in which he delivered them from the hands of the oppressors. How he had worked his signs in Egypt, and his wonders in the field along the way, and had changed their rivers into blood, and their rains, so they could not drink. He sent against them the dog-fly, and it devoured them, and the frog, and it ruined them. He gave their fruit to the cankerworm and their labors to the locust. He killed their vines with hail and their sycamores with frost. He gave up their livestock to hail, and their property to the fire. He sent out against them the fury of his anger, anger, indignation, and affliction, a message delivered by evil messengers. He made a way for his anger, and he did not spare their minds from death, but consigned their livestock to death, and struck every firstborn in the land of Egypt, including the first fruits of their labors in the tents of Ham.[3]

He moved his people like sheep and led them like a flock through the wilderness. He guided them with hope, and they were not afraid when the sea covered their enemies. He brought them into the mountain of his sanctuary, this mountain which his right hand had purchased. He drove out the nations from before them and made them inherit by a line of inheritance, and made the tribes of Israel live in their tents. Yet they tempted and provoked the Highest God, and did not keep his testimonies. They turned back, and broke the covenant, exactly as their fathers had, and they became like a crooked bow.

They provoked him in their altars[4] and moved him to jealousy with their carved statues. God heard and overlooked them, and hated Israel greatly. He rejected the tabernacle as Shiloh, his tabernacle where he lived among men.

He gave their strength into captivity and their beauty into the enemy's hand. He abandoned his people to the sword and disdained his inheritance. Fire devoured their young men, and their virgins did not mourn. Their priests were killed by the sword, and their widows were not wept for.

Then the Lord awoke as one out of sleep, and as a mighty man who had been intoxicated with wine. He slaughtered his enemies from behind, and he brought on them a perpetual reproach. He rejected the tabernacle of Joseph, and did not choose the tribe of Ephraim, but chose the tribe of Judah, and he loved Mount Zion. He built his sanctuary like the place in the heights,[5] and he founded it forever on the earth.

He chose David as his servant and took him up from the flocks of sheep. He took him from following the ewes with young, to be the shepherd of Jacob his servant, and Israel his inheritance. He tended them in the innocence of his heart and guided them by the skillfulness of his hands.

Psalms: Chapter 77 Notes

1 Codex Vacticanus: taneôs (ΤΑΝΕѠϹ). Translation: along the way

- Aleppo Codex: ṣôn (צֹעַן)
- Leningrad Codex: tz'n (צֹעַן)
- Targum to Psalms: ṭānês (טָאנֵיס). Translation: Tanis

The city of Tanis was a major city in northeast Egypt in ancient times, located in the Nile Delta along the now dried-up Tanitic branch of the Nile. The city of Tanis was identified in the classical era as the location of Zoan, the city where Moses was found in the marshes, and therefore this line of texts is often translated as Tanis in translations of the Septuagint that use the Masoretic texts for a reference. However, translating taneôs (τανεωσ) as Tanis is problematic as the Greek spelling of Tanis was Tanis (Τάνις), and certainly, the translators working in Alexandria would have known that. It is also problematic as it would then be referencing completely unknown miracles that would have taken place in Tanis, whereas translating taneôs as "along the way" makes sense in relation to both its context in this psalm and the story told in the Torah. It does, however, raise the issue of where the Masorites got the word Zoan from, as it implies they had translated their copy of this psalm from the Greek Septuagint into Hebrew and substituted the word Zoan for taneôs based on the belief at the time that Tanis was the location of the unknown city of Zoan. Those who currently view the story of Moses as a real event generally prefer the marshes of the Fayyum over the Nile, as the Fayyum was close to On (later Heliopolis) and Memphis (now part of Cairo), where the pharaoh's family was known to spend most of their time.

2 Codex Vacticanus: phôtismô pyros (ϕⲱⲧⲓⲥⲙⲱⲡⲨⲣⲟⲥ). Translation: fire lightning

• Codex Sinaiticus: phôtismô phôtos (ϕⲱⲧⲓⲥⲙⲱ ϕⲱⲧⲟⲥ). Translation: fire light

• Aleppo Codex: åûr åš (אוּר אֵש). Translation: light (or fire) fire

• Leningrad Codex: ovr esh (אוֹר אֵש). Translation: light (or fire) fire

• Targum to Psalms: nehôr ešā (נְהוֹר אֶשָׁא). Translation: light fire

3 Codex Vacticanus: Cham (ⲭⲁⲙ)
• Aleppo Codex: ḥm (חֹם)
• Leningrad Codex: cham (חָם)
• Targum to Psalms: hām (חָם)

The Hebrew term Ham appears to be a reference to the dark-skinned peoples of Africa and Southern Asia, much like the Greek word Aethiopian. It probably originated in the

Egyptian name Imåm (𓏏𓈙𓂋𓈙), which was a prominent Nubian tribe throughout the Old, Middle, and New Kingdoms.

The reference to Egypt being part of the land of Ham suggests that this psalm was composed during the Nubian rule of Egypt, between 744 and 656 BC when Egypt was part of the Empire of Kush, based in modern Sudan. If so it would have been composed during the rule of kings Jotham, Ahaz, Hezekiah, or Manasseh if composed in Judah, or during the rule of king Shallum, Pekahiah, Pekah, or Hoshea if composed in Samaria, or later under the Assyrian rule of Samaria. This reference to Egypt as the land of Ham was repeated in Psalms 104 and 105, implying that it was also written at this time.

4 Codex Vacticanus: bounoes (ΒΟΥΝΟΙϹ). Translation: altars (or heaps, mounds)

• Aleppo Codex: bmûtm (בָּמוֹתָם). Translation: bamas (altars on hilltops)

• Leningrad Codex: vamotam (בָּמוֹתָם). Translation: bamas (altars on hilltops)

5 Codex Vaticanus: monocerôtôn (ΜΟΝΟΚΕΡωΤωΝ). Translation: unicorns

• Septuagint manuscript 55: monocerôton (μονοκέροτον). Translation: unicorns

• Septuagint manuscript 1219: monocerôtos (ΜΟΝΟΚΕΡωΤΟϹ). Translation: unicorn

• Alpha Codex: rmym (רמים). Translation: heights

- Leningrad Codex: ramim (רָמִים). Translation: heights
- Vetus Latina manuscripts: unicornum. Translation: unicorn
- Targum to Psalms: rîmenā (רִימְנָא). Translation: heights

The differences between the Greek and Hebrew translations suggest the term rmym (רמים) was misread as râmym (ראמים) at some point. It is unlikely that the original verse was "He built his sanctuary like the place of rhinoceroses," and so the Masoretic term "heights" is imported.

Psalms: Chapter 78

A Psalm for Asaph.

God, the foreigners have come into your inheritance. They have polluted your holy temple. They have made Jerusalem a storehouse of fruits. They have given the dead bodies of your servants to be food for the birds of the sky, the flesh of your holy ones for the wild beasts of the earth. They shed their blood like water around Jerusalem, and there was no one to bury them.

We have become an insult to our neighbors, an insult and derision to those who are around us. How long, Lord? Will you be angry forever? Will your jealousy burn like fire? Pour out your anger on the foreigners that have not known you, and on the kingdoms which have not called on your name.

For they have devoured Jacob and laid his place waste. Don't remember our old transgressions. Let your tender mercies speedily prevent us, for we are greatly impoverished. Help us, God our Savior, for the glory of your name, Lord, deliver us and be merciful to our sins for your name's sake.

If they should say among the foreigners, "Where is their God?" Let the avenging of your servant's blood that has been shed, be known among the foreigners before our eyes. Let the groaning of the prisoners come in before you, and according to the greatness of your arm preserve the men appointed to die. Repay to our neighbors seven times into their chest their insult, with which they have insulted you, Lord. For we are your people and the sheep of your pasture, and we will give you thanks forever, and we will declare your praise throughout all generations.

Psalms: Chapter 79

For the end, for alternate strains. A testimony for Asaph. A psalm concerning the Assyrians.

Pay attention, Shepherd of Israel, who guides Joseph like a flock. You who rides on the sphinx, shine on Ephraim and Benjamin and Manasseh, stir up your power, and come to deliver us. Return to us, God, and make your face shine, and we will be saved. Lord the god Sabaoth, how long have you been angry with the prayer of your servant?

You will feed us with the bread of tears and will cause us to drink tears by measure. You have made us a strife to our neighbors, and our enemies have mocked us. Return to us, Lord, the god Sabaoth, and cause your face to shine, and we will be saved.

Separate the psalm.

You have transplanted a vine out of Egypt. You have thrown out the nations and replanted it. You made a way before it and caused its roots to strike, and the land was filled with it. Its shadow covered the mountains, and its shoots equaled the cedars of God. It sent out its branches to the sea, and its shoots to the river. Why have you broken down its hedge, while all who pass along the way pluck it?

The boar out of the woods has laid it waste, and the wild beast has devoured it. God Sabaoth, return, we beg you. Look on us from the sky, and look and visit this vine, and restore that which your right hand has planted, and look on the son of man whom you strengthened for yourself. It is burnt with fire and dug up, and they will perish at the rebuke of your presence.

Let your hand be on the man, and your right hand on the son of man whom you did strengthen for yourself, so we will not leave you. You will quicken us, and we will call on your name. Return to us, Lord the god Sabaoth, and make your face shine, and we will be saved.

Psalms: Chapter 80

For the end. A psalm for Asaph.[1] Concerning the wine presses.

Rejoice in God our helper, and cry aloud to the God of Jacob. Take a psalm, and produce the timbrel, the pleasant lute with the harp. Blow the trumpet at the new moon, on the glorious day of your feast. For this is an ordinance for Israel and a statute of the God of Jacob. He made it as a testimony in Joseph when he came out of the land of Egypt, and he heard a language that he did not understand. He removed his back from burdens, and his hands slaved in making the baskets. You called on me in trouble, and I delivered you, and I heard you in the secret place of the storm. I tested you at the water of contradiction.

Separate the psalm.

Listen, my people, and I will speak to you, Israel, and I will testify to you. If you will listen to me there will be no new god among you. Nor will you worship a foreign god. For I am the Lord your god, who brought you out of the land of Egypt. Open your mouth wide, and I will fill it. But my people did not listen to my voice, and Israel did not obey me. So I let them go after the ways of their hearts. They will go on in their ways. If my people had listened to me, if Israel had walked in my ways, I should have put down their enemies very quickly and should have laid my hand on those who afflicted them. The Lord's enemies should have lied to him, but their time will be forever. He fed them with the oil of wheat and satisfied them with honey out of the rock.

Psalms: Chapter 80 Notes

1 Codex Vatianus: Asaph (ⲁⲥⲁⲫ). Translation: Asaph
- Codex Sinaiticus: Dauid (ⲇⲁⲩⲉⲓⲇ). Translation: David
- Aleppo Codex: åsp (אֹסְף). Translation: Asaph
- Leningrad Codex: asaf (אָסָף). Translation: Asaph
- Targum to Psalms: āsāp (אָסָף). Translation: height

The Codex Sinaiticus states that this is a psalm for David, not Asaph.

Psalms: Chapter 81

A Psalm for Asaph.

God stands in the assembly of the gods,[1] and among the gods, he will judge. How long will you judge unrighteously, and accept the bodies of sinners?

Separate the psalm.

Judge the orphan and poor. Do justice to the low and needy. Rescue the needy, and deliver the poor out of the hand of the sinner. They don't know or understand. They walk on in darkness. All the foundations of the earth will be shaken. I have said, "You are gods, and all of you are children of the Highest. But you die like men, and fall like one of the princes."

Rise, God, judge the earth, for you will inherit all nations.

Psalms: Chapter 81 Notes

1 Codex Vacticanus: o theos estê en synagôgê theôn (Ο ΘΕΟC ΕCΤΗ ΕΝ CΥΝΑΓΩΓΗ ΘΕΩΝ). Translation: the god stands in the assembly of gods

• Dead Sea Scroll MasPsᵃ: ålhym nṣb bôdt-ål (אלהים נצב בעדת-אל). Translation: goddesses (in Hebrew, or gods in Aramaic, or God in Neo-Assyrian) stands in the congregation of God

• Aleppo Codex: ålhym nṣb bôdt-ål (אלהים נצב בעדת-אל).
Translation: goddesses (in Hebrew, or gods in Aramaic, or God
in Neo-Assyrian) stands in the congregation of God

• Leningrad Codex: elohim nitzav ba'adat-el (נִצָּב אֱלֹהִים
בַּעֲדַת־אֵל). Translation: goddesses (in Hebrew, or gods in Aramaic, or God in Neo-Assyrian) stands in the congregation of
God

Psalms: Chapter 82

A song of a psalm for Asaph.

God, who will be compared to you? Do not be silent, nor be still, God. For look, your enemies have made a noise, and those who hate you have lifted their heads. Against your people, they have cunningly imagined a plan, and have taken counsel against your holy ones. They have said, "Come, and let's completely exterminate them out of the nation, and let the name of Israel be remembered no longer."

They have taken counsel together with one consent, and they have made an alliance against you, including the tents of the Edomites, Ishmaelites, Moabites, Hagrites,[1] Byblosians,[2] Ammonites, nomads,[3] and the nations also, along with those who live in Tyre. Yes, Assyria also has come with them, and they have become an ally to the children of Lot.

Separate the psalm.

Do to them like Midian, and like Sisera, and like Jabin at the brook of Kishion. They were completely destroyed at Endor, and they became like dung for the earth. Make their princes like Oreb, Zeeb, Zebee, and Zalmunna. Including all their princes who said, "Let us take to ourselves the sanctuary of God as an inheritance."

My God, make them like a wheel, and as stubble before the face of the wind. As fire which will burn up wood, as the flame may consume the mountains, so will you persecute them with your tempest, and trouble them in your anger. Fill their faces with dishonor, and so they will seek your name, Lord. Let them be ashamed and troubled forever. Yes, let them be confused and destroyed. Let them know that your name is the Lord and that you alone are Highest over all the earth.

Psalms: Chapter 82 Notes

1 Codex Vacticanus: Angarênoe (ΑΓΓΑΡΗΝΟΙ)
* Septuagint manuscript 55: Agarênoe (Αγάβληνοι)

* Dead Sea Scroll MasPsᵃ: hgrym (הגרים)
* Aleppo Codex: hgrym (הגרים)
* Leningrad Codex: hagrim (הַגְרִים)
* Targum to Psalms: hûnegrāê (הוּנְגְרָאֵי). Translation: Hungarians

The Hagrites were recorded as a nomadic tribe living east of Samaria in 1ˢᵗ Paralipomenon.

2 Codex Vacticanus: Naebal (ΝΑΙΒΑΛ)
* Papyrus Oxyrhynchus 1352 (LXX 2049): Gaeba (ΓΑΙΒΑ)
* Dead Sea Scroll MasPsᵃ: gbl (גבל)
* Aleppo Codex: gbl (גבל)
* Leningrad Codex: gvl (גבל)

- Sahidic manuscripts: Ueber (γεвер)
- Vetus Latina manuscripts: Geban
- Targum to Psalms: gûbelāê (גּוּבְלָאֵי). Translation: Jablehians (جَبْلَاوِي)

Gebal is the ancient Canaanite and Hebrew name for the city of Byblos in Lebanon. The city was known as Kbn (ﮐﺒﻦ) by the Egyptians since the Old Kingdom era, and Gbl (𐤊𐤁𐤋) by the Ugaritic Canaanites in the 1300s BC. The modern Arabic name Jibayl (جبيل) is derived from the name Gbl. The Greek name Býblos (Βύβλος) was derived from the word for papyrus, which the city was a major exporter of early in Greek civilization. The Greek, Coptic, and Latin versions of this name are inconsistent, however, some may be transliteration errors of the Aramaic name Gbl (ܓܒܠ), and therefore the name from the Masoretic texts is imported.

3 Codex Vaticanus: amalêc (ΑΜΑΛΗΚ)
- Aleppo Codex: ômlq (עֲמָלִק)
- Leningrad Codex: amalek (עֲמָלֵק)
- Targum to Psalms: Araba'ei (עַרְבָאֵי). Translation: Arabs

In the Israelite books, the Amalek are periodically present in southern Canaan and the Sinai peninsula from the time of Moses until the time of King David, however, there is no archeological evidence of a tribe called Amalek. The name is a transliteration of the Egyptian term âmǔ lqî (𓀭𓀭𓏏𓈖 𓂝𓈖), which can be translated as "hostile Asiatics," "opposing Amorites," or "defiant fires."

An Egyptian named Ahmose pen-Nekhbet reported fighting at Avaris and Sharuhen in the autobiography craved into his tomb around the time of Moses' Exodus. He also noted that the Egyptians fought the šåsů (𓈙𓄿𓂧𓏭𓏭), meaning "nomads," in the Sinai peninsula during these campaigns. These nomads do not appear to have been the Israelites, who according to the Israelite texts would have been deep in the wilderness east of Edom by that point. However, the book of Numbers also places the "hostile Asiatics" in the Negev, which is where the Egyptians fought the nomads, indicating these were the same people. In the time of David, the term still referred to the nomadic tribes that lived in Midian, the Negev, and the Sinai peninsula. Therefore, this translation uses the term "nomads," as that appears to be the original meaning.

Psalms: Chapter 83

A psalm for the sons of Korah. Concerning the wine presses.

How amiable are your tabernacles, Lord Sabaoth! My mind longs and faints for the courts of the Lord. My heart and my flesh have celebrated in the living god. Yes, the sparrow has found himself a home, and the turtle-dove a nest for herself, where she may lay her young, even your altars, Lord Sabaoth, my king, and my god. Blessed are those who live in your temple, they will praise you forever.

Separate the psalm.

Blessed is the man whose help is from you, Lord, and in his heart, he has purposed to go up the valley of weeping, to the place which he has appointed, for there the law-giver will grant blessings. They will go from strength to strength. The god of gods will be seen in Zion. Lord the god Sabaoth, hear my prayer, listen to the god of Jacob!

Separate the psalm.

Look, God, our defender, and see the face of your anointed. For one day in your courts is better than thousands. I would rather be an abject in the temple of God than live in the tents of sinners. The Lord loves mercy and truth. God will give grace and glory. The Lord will

not withhold good things from those who walk in innocence. Lord Sabaoth, blessed is the man who trusts in
you.

Psalms: Chapter 84

A psalm for the sons of Korah.

Lord, you have taken pleasure in your land. You have turned back the captivity of Jacob. You have forgiven your people for their transgressions. You have covered all their sins.

Separate the psalm.

You have caused all your anger to cease. You have turned from your fierce anger. Return to us, the god of our salvation, and turn your anger away from us. Would you be angry with us forever? Or will you continue your anger from generation to generation? God, you will turn and quicken us, and your people will rejoice in you. Show us your mercy, Lord, and grant us your salvation. I will hear what Lord the god will say concerning me. For he will speak peace to his people, and his saints, and to those who turn their heart towards him.

Moreover, his salvation is near those who fear him, and that glory may live in our land. Mercy and truth are met together, and righteousness and peace have kissed each other. Truth has sprung out of the earth, and righteousness has looked down from the sky. The Lord will give goodness, and our land will yield her fruit. Righteousness will go before him and will set his steps in the way.

Psalms: Chapter 85

A Prayer of David.

Lord, incline your ear, and listen to me, for I am poor and needy. Preserve my mind, for I am holy. Save your servant, God, he who hopes in you. Pity me, Lord, for to you will I cry all day. Rejoice in the mind of your servant, for to the Lord have I lifted my mind. For you, Lord, are kind, gentle, and plenteous in mercy to all who call on you. Give ear to my prayer, Lord, and attend to the voice of my supplication. On the day of my trouble, I cried to you, for you heard me. There is none like you, Lord, among the gods, and there are no works like your works.

All nations whom you have made will come and will worship before you, Lord, and will glorify your name. For you are great and do wonders. You are the only great god. Guide me, Lord, in your way, and I will walk in your truth. Let my heart rejoice, that I may fear your name. I will thank you, Lord, my god, with all my heart, and I will glorify your name forever. For your mercy is great towards me, and you have delivered my mind from the bottom of Sheol. God, transgressors have risen up against me, and an assembly of violent men have wanted my life, and have not set you before them.

But you, Lord the god, are compassionate and merciful, patient, and abundant in mercy and truth. Look on me, and have mercy on me, and give your strength to your servant, and save the son of your slave woman. Establish with me a token for good, and let those who hate me see it and be ashamed, because you, Lord, have helped me, and comforted me.

Psalms: Chapter 86

A psalm of a Song for the sons of Korah.

His foundations are in the holy mountains. The Lord loves the gates of Zion, more than all the tabernacles of Jacob. Glorious things have been spoken of you, the city of God.

Separate the psalm.

I will make mention of Egypt[1] and Babylon to those who know me, and also see the nations, and Tyre, and the Kushite peoples. These were born there. A man will say, "Zion is my mother," and such a man was born in her, and the Highest himself has founded her. The Lord will recount it in the writing of the people, and of these princes that have been in her. The living of all within you is like the living of those who rejoice.

Psalms: Chapter 86 Notes

1 Codex Vacticanus: Raab (ΡΑΑΒ)

• Aleppo Codex: rhb (רהב). Translation: proud, splendid, bluster, Rahab

• Leningrad Codex: rahav (רְהַב). Translation: proud, splendid, bluster, Rahab

• Targum to Psalms: miṣrāê (מִצְרָאִי). Translation: Egypt

The Greek term was a direct transliteration of the Hebrew term rhb (רהב), however, at other points, the Greeks translated rhb (רהב) as Cetus (κήτη), such as in Job. Rehob is also likely the source of the name Rêchab (Ρηχαβ) in Judges chapter 1. Rehob is a Hebrew term that refers to a sea monster, possibly a synonym for Lotan / Leviathan. It also became a synonym for "pride," and is generally interpreted for the domain of the Pharaoh, who wore a crown shaped like a cobra's head. In Judges, chapter 1, Rêchab (Ρηχαβ) is reported to have stopped the Israelites' conquest of Canaan, which does correspond with the army of Egypt marching through Canaan and pacifying it in the same year according to the Septuagint's chronology. Based on the context in this verse, a country is being referenced, and so the name Egypt is used.

Psalms: Chapter 87

A song of a psalm for the sons of Korah. For the end, on Mahalath for responsive strains. Of understanding for Aeman the Israelite.

Lord the god, my salvation, I have cried by day and in the night before you. Let my prayer come in before you, listen to my supplication, Lord. For my mind is filled with troubles, and my life has drawn near to Sheol. I have been reckoned with those who go down to the pit, and I became like a man without help, and free among the dead, like the slain ones that were abandoned and who sleep in the tomb, who you remember no longer, as they are rejected from your hand. They laid me in the lowest pit, in dark places, and in the shadow of Mot.[1] Your anger has pressed heavily on me, and you have brought on me all your billows.

Separate the psalm.

You have removed my acquaintance far from me, and they have made me an abomination to themselves. I have been delivered up, and have not gone out. My eyes are dimmed from poverty, but I cried to you, Lord, all the days, and I spread forth my hands to you. Will you work wonders for the dead? Will physicians raise them, those who will praise you? Will anyone declare your mercy from the tomb, and your truth in Abaddon?[2] Will your wonders be known in the darkness, and your righteousness in a forgotten land?

I cried to you, Lord, and in the morning my prayer will reach up to you. Therefore, Lord, do you reject my prayer, and turn your face away from me? I am poor and in trouble from my youth, and having been praised, I was brought low and into despair. Your anger has passed over me, and your terrors have greatly disquieted me. They surrounded me like water, and all day they beset me together. You have put far from me every friend, and my acquaintances because of my wretchedness.

Psalms: Chapter 87 Notes

1 Codex Vacticanus: en scotinoes cae en scia thanatou (ƐN CKOTEINOIC KAI ƐN CKIⱯ ⲞⱯNⱯTOY). Translation: in darkness and in the shadow of Thanatos (or death)

• Aleppo Codex: bmslût (בְּמַצְלוֹת). Translation: in the shade covered

• Leningrad Codex: bimtzolot (בְּמַצְלְוֹת). Translation: in the shade covered

• Targum to Psalms: ůehinûn mēappê šekintāk itpalāgûn (וְהִנוּן מֵאַפֵּי שְׁכִנְתָּךְ אִתְפַּלָגוּן). Translation: and among the darkened (or gloom) abode (or dwelling place) of the departed

The Greek translation indicates that the Aramaic text was different from the Hebrew and Judeo-Aramaic translations.

Unfortunately, this verse does not survive among any of the Dead Sea Scrolls for comparision. As the "shadow of Thanatos" (θανατου) is previously mirrored by "shadow of Mot" (מות) in chapter 22, that name is restored here.

2 Codex Vacticanus: apôlia (ΑΠⲰⲖⲈⲒΑ). Translation: destruction (or loss)

• Aleppo Codex: âbdûn (אבדון). Translation: devastation (or doom, ruin)

• Leningrad Codex: avaddon (אֲבַדּוֹן). Translation: devastation (or doom, ruin)

• Targum to Psalms: ābedānā (אֲבְדָנָא). Translation: ruin (or destruction)

The term Abaddon is debated. The term is either a place or the name of a being of some king in Proverbs and Job. The Second Temple era Thanksgiving Hymns, found within the Dead Sea Scrolls, treats it as the name of the underworld. Abaddon is an angel in the Gnostic-Christian Revelation of John, resulting in various Christian denominations interpreting Abaddon as either an angel or archangel of god, or an angel of Satan, or sometimes the angelic name of Jesus. In the Gnostic-Christian Acts of Thomas it was the name of a demon, while in the Gnostic-Christian Book of the Resurrection of Jesus Christ, it was the name of the guardian angel of humanity, who was present at the resurrection of Jesus.

The Mandean Ginza Rabba also treats it as the name of the underworld, divided into an Upper Abaddon and a Lower

Abaddon. As the name Abaddon was almost certainly the name that the Greeks translated as apôlia, the name is restored in this translation from the Masoretic text.

Psalms: Chapter 88

A psalm of instruction for Ethan the Israelite.

I will sing of your mercies, Lord, forever. I will declare your truth with my mouth to all generations, for you have said, "Mercy will be built up forever. Your truth will be established in the sky. I made a covenant with my chosen ones, I swore to David, my servant. I will prepare your seed forever, and build up your throne to all generations."

Separate the psalm.

The sky will declare your wonders, Lord, and your truth in the assembly of the saints. For who in the clouds will be compared to the Lord? Who will be compared to the Lord among the sons of God? God is glorified in the council of the saints, great and terrible towards all that are around him. Lord the god Sabaoth, who is like you? You are mighty, Lord, and your truth is around you. You rule the power of the sea, and you calm the tumult of its waves. You have brought down the proud like one that is slain, and with the arm of your power, you have scattered your enemies. The sky is yours, and the earth is yours. You have created the world and the fullness of it. You have created the north and the sea. Tabor and Hermon will rejoice in your name.

Yours is a mighty arm, and let your hand be strengthened, let your right hand be praised. Justice and judgment are the establishments of your throne. Mercy and truth will go before your face. Blessed are the people who know the joyful sound, and they will walk, Lord, in the light of your countenance. In your name will they rejoice all the day, and in your righteousness will they be praised. For you are the boast of their strength, and in your good pleasure will our horn be praised, for our help is from the Lord, and the Holy One of Israel, our king.

Then you spoke in a vision to your children, and said, "I have laid help on a mighty one, I have praised one chosen out of my people. I have found David my servant, and I have anointed him by my holy mercy. My hand will support him, and my arm will strengthen him. The enemy will have no advantage against him, and the son of transgression will not hurt him again. I will cut down his enemies before him and put to flight those who hate him. My truth and my mercy will be with him, and in my name will his horn be praised. I will set his hand in the sea, and his right hand in the rivers.

He will call on me, saying, "You are my Father, my God, and the helper of my salvation." I will make him my firstborn, higher than the kings of the earth. I will keep my mercy for him forever, and my covenant will be firm with him. I will establish his descendants forever and ever, and his throne like the days of the sky. If his children should forget my law, and not follow my judgments, if they should profane my ordinances, and not keep my commandments, I will visit their transgressions with a wand, and their sins with scourges. But my mercy I will not completely remove from him, or invalidate my truth. Nor will I by any means profane my covenant, and I will not make void the things that proceed out of my lips. Once I have sworn by my holiness, that I will not lie to David, his seed will endure forever, and his throne as the sun before me, and as the moon that is established forever, and as the faithful witness in the sky.

Separate the psalm.

But you have thrown it away and set at nothing, you have rejected your anointed. You have overthrown the covenant of your servant, and you have profaned his sanctuary, throwing it to the ground. You have broken down all his hedges, and you have made his strongholds a terror. All who travel by the road have plundered him, he has become a reproach to his neighbors. You have praised the right hand of his enemies, and you have made all his enemies rejoice. You have turned back the help of his sword, and have not helped him in the battle. You have deprived him of purification, and you have broken down his throne to the ground. You have shortened the days of his throne. You have poured shame on him.

Separate the psalm.

How long, Lord, will you turn away? Forever? Will your anger burn out like fire? Remember what my being is, for have you created all the sons of Adam in vain? What man is there who will live, and not see death? Will anyone deliver his mind from the hand of Sheol?

Separate the psalm.

Where are your ancient mercies, Lord, which you swore to David in your truth? Remember, Lord, the reproach of your servants, which I have borne in my bosom, even the reproach of many nations, where your enemies have criticized, Lord,[1] and where they have criticized the repay of your anointed. Blessed is the Lord forever. So be it, so be it.

Psalms: Chapter 88 Notes

1 Codex Vacticanus: cyrie (ΚΥΡΙΕ). Translation: sir (or lord)

• Dead Sea Scroll 4QPsᵉ: ădůny (אדוני). Translation: "my lord."

• Aleppo Codex: yhůh (יהוה)

• Leningrad Codex: yehvah (יְהֹוָה)

- Targum to Psalms: yeyā (יְיָ)

The Greek translation uses the term cyrie (κύριε), meaning, "sir," or "lord," indicating the Aramaic text used either the term bôlå (ܢܠܥܝ) or ådny (ܐܕܢܝ), which the Hebrew translators replaced with Yahweh. Dead Sea Scroll 4QPsᵉ confirms that ådůny (אדוני) was translated into at least some Hebrew copies as late as the Herodian Period, meaning the Hebrew translations of Psalms were still not standardized by that era.

As there is no evidence of Yhůh being in Psalms before Simon's Hebrew translation, and the Dead Sea Scroll 4QPsᵉ confirms the Greek translation, Lord is translated from cyrie (κύριε).

Psalms: Chapter 89

A prayer of Moses prophet.

Lord, you have been our refuge in all generations. Before the mountains existed, and before the earth and the world were formed, even from age to age, you are. Turn not man back to his low place, whereas you said, "Return, you sons of Adam." A thousand years in your sight are like yesterday, which has just passed, and as a watch in the night. Years will be their vanities. Let the morning pass away like grass. In the morning let it flower, and pass away, and in the evening let it droop, let it be withered and dried up, for we have perished in your anger, and in your anger, we have been troubled.

You have set our transgressions before you, and our age is in the light of your countenance. For all our days are gone, and we have passed away in your anger, and our years have mediated their tale like a spider. As for the days of our years, in them are seventy years, and if men should be in strength, eighty years. The greater part of them would be labor and trouble, for weakness overtakes us, and we will be punished. Who knows the power of your anger? Who knows how to number his days because of the fear of your anger? So manifest your right hand and those who are instructed in wisdom in the heart. Return, Lord, how long? Be begged concerning your servants. We have been satisfied in the morning with your mercy, and we did celebrate and rejoice. Let us rejoice in all our days, in return for the days in which you did afflict us, the years in which we saw evil.

Look at your servants, and your works, and guide their children. Let the brightness of Lord the god be on us, and make the works of our hands prosper.

Psalms: Chapter 90

Praise of a Song, by David.

He who lives with the help of the Highest will stay under the shelter of the god of the sky.[1] He will say to the Lord, "You are my helper and my refuge, my god, and I will trust in him. For he will deliver you from the snare of the hunters, from every troublesome matter. He will overshadow you with his shoulders, and you will trust under his wings, and his truth will cover you with a shield. You will not be afraid of the terror by night, nor of the arrow flying by day, nor of the evil thing that walks in darkness, nor of calamity, and the evil spirit at noon-day. A thousand will fall at your side, and ten thousand at your right hand, but it will not come near you. Only with your eyes will you observe and see the reward of sinners."

For you, Lord, are my hope, and you have made the Highest your refuge. No evils will come on you, and no scourge will draw near to your living, for he will give his messengers charge concerning you, to keep you in all your ways. They will carry you upon their hands, in case at any time you dash your foot against a stone. You will tread on the asp and basilisk, and you will trample on the lions and dragons. For he has trusted in me, and I will deliver him, and I will protect him because he has known my name. He will call on me, and I will listen to him. I am with him in affliction, and I will deliver him, and glorify him. I will satisfy him with a length of days and show him my salvation.

Psalms: Chapter 90 Notes

1 Codex Vacticanus: theoú toú ouranoú (ΘΕΟΥΤΟΥ ΟΥΡΑΝΟΥ). Translation: god of the vaulted sky (or Uranus)

• Dead Sea Scroll Apocryphal Psalms: -šdy (‎-שׁדי). Translation: -Shaddai

• Aleppo Codex: bṣl šdy (‎בצל שׁדי). Translation: the shadow of Shaddai (or demonic, mischievous, malicious)

• Leningrad Codex: betzel shaddai (‎בְּצֵל שַׁדִּי). Translation: the shadow of Shaddai (or demonic, mischievous, malicious)

• Targum to Psalms: berāzā ilāâ (‎בְּרָזָא עִלָּאָה). Translation: orifice ascended

Psalms: Chapter 91

A psalm of a Song for the Sabbath.

It is a good thing to give thanks to the Lord, and to sing praises to your name, Highest, to proclaim your mercy in the morning, and your truth by night, on a lute of ten strings, with a song on the harp. For you, The Lord has made me happy with your work, and in the operations of your hands will I celebrate. How your works have been praised, Lord! Your thoughts are very deep. A foolish man will not know, and a senseless man will not understand this.

When the sinners spring up as the grass, all the workers of iniquity have watched and it is they who may be annihilated forever. But you, Lord, are Highest forever, for, look, your enemies will die and all the workers of iniquity will be scattered. But my horn will be praised like the horn of a rhinoceros and my old age with rich mercy. My eye has seen my enemies, and my ear will hear the wicked who rise up against me. The righteous will flourish like a palm tree. He will be increased like the cedar in Lebanon.

They who are planted in the temple of the Lord and will flourish in the courts of our god. Then will they be increased in a fat old age, and they will be prosperous, and that they may declare that the Lord my god is righteous, and there is no iniquity in him.

Psalms: Chapter 92

For the day before the Sabbath, when the land was first inhabited. The praise of a song by David.

The Lord reigns and he has clothed himself with honor! The Lord has clothed and girded himself with strength, for he has established the world, which is immovable. Your ancient throne is prepared, and you are from eternity. The rivers have lifted, Lord, the rivers have lifted their voices, at the voices of many waters. The billows of the sea are wonderful, and the Lord is wonderful in high places. Your testimonies are made very sure, and holiness becomes your temple, Lord, for a length of days.

Psalms: Chapter 93

A psalm of David for the fourth day of the week.

The Lord is a god of vengeance. The god of vengeance has declared himself. Be praised, you that judge the earth. Render a reward to the proud. How long will sinners, Lord, how long will sinners boast? They will talk, and speak unrighteousness, and all the workers of iniquity will speak so. They have afflicted your people, Lord, and hurt your heritage. They have slain the widow and fatherless and murdered the stranger. They said, "The Lord will not see, neither will the God of Jacob understand."

Understand now, you simple among the people, and you fools, at eventually become wise. He who planted his ear, does he not hear? He who formed the eye, does not he perceive? He who chastises the nations, will he not punish? He who teaches man knowledge? The Lord knows the thoughts of men, that they are vain.

Blessed is the man whoever you will punish, Lord, and will teach him out of your law to give him rest from evil days, until a pit is dug for the sinful one. The Lord will not throw away his people, neither will he forget his inheritance, until righteousness returns to judgment, and all the upright in heart will follow it.

Separate the psalm.

Who will rise up for me against the transgressors? Who will stand up with me against the workers of iniquity? If the Lord had not helped me, my mind would have almost stayed in Sheol. If I said, "My foot has been moved, your mercy, Lord, helped me. Lord, according to the multitude of my griefs within my heart, your consolation has loved my mind. Will the throne of iniquity have fellowship with you, which frames plans by an ordinance?

They will hunt for the mind of the righteous and condemn innocent blood. But the Lord was my refuge, and my god the helper of my hope. He will repay to them their iniquity and their iniquity, the Lord our god will completely destroy them.

Psalms: Chapter 94

A Praise Song by David.

Come, let us celebrate to the Lord, and let us make a joyful noise to God our savior. Let's come before his presence with thanksgiving, and make a joyful noise to him with psalms. For the Lord is a great god, and a great king over all gods.[1] The Lord will not abandon his people. For the edges of the earth are in his hands, and the heights of the mountains are his. For the sea is his, and he made it. His hands formed the desert. Come, let us worship and fall down before him, and cry before the Lord who made us. For he is our God, and we are the people of his pasture, and the sheep of his hand, today, if you will hear his voice, harden not your hearts, as in the provocation, according to the day of irritation in the wilderness where your fathers tempted me, proved me, and saw my works. Forty years was I grieved with this generation, and said, "They do always err in their heart, and they have not known my ways. So I swore in my anger, 'They will not enter into my rest.'"

Psalms: Chapter 94 Notes

1 Codex Vacticanus: basileus megas epi pantas tous theous (ΒΑϹΙΛΕΥϹ ΜΕΓΑϹ ΕΠΙ ΠΑΝΤΑϹ ΤΟΥϹ ΘΕΟΥϹ). Translation: great king of all gods

• Codex Alexandrinus: basileus megas epi pantas tous theous (ΒΑΣΙΛΕΥΣ ΜΕΓΑΣ ΕΠΙ ΠΑΣΑΝ ΤΗΝ ΓΗΝ). Translation: great king in all the land

• Dead Sea Scroll 4QPs^m: -ym (ים-). Most of the letters in the phrase are missing.

• Aleppo Codex: ål gdůl yhůh ůmlk gdůl ôl-kl-ålhym (אל גדול יהוה ומלך גדול על-כל-אלהים). Translation: God the great the Yahweh and great king on all gods

• Leningrad Codex: el gadovl yehvah umelech gadovl al-kol-elohim (אֵל גָּדוֹל יְהוָה וּמֶלֶךְ גָּדוֹל עַל־כָּל־אֱלֹהִים). Translation: to the great the Yehvah and great king on all gods

Psalms: Chapter 95

When the temple was built after the captivity, a Song of David.

Sing to the Lord a new song! Sing to the Lord, all the earth. Sing to the Lord, bless his name, and proclaim his salvation from day to day. Publish his glory among the nations, his wonderful works among all people. The Lord is great and greatly to be praised, and he is more terrible than all the gods. For all the gods of the foreigners are demons, but the Lord made the sky. Thanksgiving and beauty are before him. Holiness and majesty are in his sanctuary.

Bring to the Lord, you families of the nations, bring to the Lord glory and honor. Bring to the Lord the glory fit for his name, and make offerings in his courts. Worship the Lord in his holy court, and let all the earth tremble before him. Say among the foreigners, "The Lord reigns! He has established the world so that it will not be moved, and he will judge the people in righteousness."

Let Shamayim rejoice, Eretz celebrate, and Yam be moved in his entirety. Shaddai[1] will rejoice, and all things in him. All the trees of the forest will celebrate before the presence of the Lord when he comes. He comes to judge the earth. He will judge the world in righteousness and the people with his truth.

Psalms: Chapter 95 Notes

1 Codex Vacticanus: pedia (ⲡⲉⲇⲓⲁ). Translation: fields (or grounds)

- Aleppo Codex: šdy (שׁדי). Translation: Shaddai (or demonic, mischievous, malicious)

- Leningrad Codex: sadai (שָׂדִי). Translation: Shaddai (or demonic, mischievous, malicious)

Psalms: Chapter 96

For David. When his land is established.

The Lord reigns! Let the earth celebrate! Let many islands rejoice. Cloud and darkness are around him, and righteousness and judgment are the establishments of his throne. Fire will go before him and burn up his enemies around. His lightning appeared to the world, and the earth saw and trembled. The mountains melted like wax in the presence of the Lord, in the presence of the Lord of the whole earth. Shamayim has declared his righteousness, and all the people have seen his glory. Let all that worship carved statues be ashamed, who boast of their idols.

Worship him, all you, his messengers. Zion heard and rejoiced, and the daughters of Judah celebrated, because of your judgments, Lord. For you are Highest over all the earth, and you are greatly praised above all gods. You who love the Lord, hate evil. The Lord preserves the minds of his saints, and he will deliver them from the hands of sinners. Light is sprung up for the righteous, and gladness for the upright in heart. Rejoice in the Lord, you righteous, and give thanks for a remembrance of his holiness.

Psalms: Chapter 97

A psalm of David.

Sing to the Lord a new song, for the Lord has worked wonderful works, his right hand, and his holy arm, have worked salvation for him. The Lord has made known his salvation, he has revealed his righteousness in the sight of the nations. He has remembered his mercy to Jacob, and his truth to the house of Israel. All the edges of the earth have seen the salvation of our god.

Shout to God, all the earth! Sing, and celebrate, and sing psalms. Sing to the Lord with a harp, with a harp, and the voice of a psalm. With trumpets of metal, and the sound of a trumpet of the horn making a joyful noise to the Lord before the king. Let the sea be moved in its entirety, and the world it exists in. The rivers[1] will clap their hands together, and the mountains[2] will celebrate, for he is come to judge the earth. He will judge the world in righteousness, and the nations in uprightness.

Psalms: Chapter 97 Notes

1 Codex Vacticanus: potamoí (ΠΟΤΑΜΟΙ). Translation: rivers

- Aleppo Codex: nhrůt (נהרות). Translation: rivers
- Leningrad Codex: neharot (נְהָרֹות). Translation: rivers
- Targum to Psalms: neharwātā (נְהַרְוָתָא). Translation: rivers

The Jordan and Tigris Rivers were often depicted as sentient beings in ancient Israelite literature, such as the Life of Adam and Eve literature. Many ancient Middle Eastern cultures believed their rivers were lesser gods, including the Assyrians who regarded the Tigris and Euphrates as deities, and the Egyptians who viewed the Nile as a deity. This reference to the Jordan being sentient is repeated in Psalm 113, implying that the authors of the Psalms may have generally viewed rivers as sentient.

2 Codex Vacticanus: orê (ΟΡΗ). Translation: mountains

- Aleppo Codex: hrym (הרים). Translation: mountains
- Leningrad Codex: harim (הָרִים). Translation: mountains
- Targum to Psalms: ṭûrayā (טוּרַיָּא). Translation: mountains

The Mountains / Ourea were primordial deities in Greek mythology, children of Earth / Ge. The Kur served the same role in the ancient Mesopotamian religions. The author of this psalm clearly believed the mountains were sentient, like the author of the Testament of Judah.

Psalms: Chapter 98

A psalm of David.

The Lord reigns![1] Let the people rage! It is he who rides on the sphinx, let the earth be moved! The Lord is great in Zion and is high over all the people. Let them give thanks to your great name, for it is terrible and holy. The king's honor loves judgment, and you have prepared equity, you have worked judgment and justice in Jacob. Celebrate the Lord our god, and worship at his footstool, for he is holy. Moses and Aaron among his priests, and Samuel among those who call on his name, and they called on the Lord, and he heard them. He spoke to them in a pillar of cloud, and they kept his testimonies and the ordinances that he gave them. Lord our god, you heard them! God, you became propitious to them, though you did take vengeance on all their plans. Celebrate the Lord our god, and worship at his holy mountain, for the Lord our god is holy.

Psalms: Chapter 98 Notes

1 Codex Vacticanus: o cyrios ebasileusen (OKYPIOC ЄΒΑΣΙΛЄΥϹЄΝ). Translation: the lord is the king

• Dead Sea Scroll 4QPs^k: ldŭ- (-ו̃ד). The damaged word in DSS 4QPs^k is accepted as having been ldŭd (לדוד), meaning "to David" in Hebrew, or "for David" in Aramaic. The term ledavid (לְדָוִד) does appear in the Masoretic texts, such as the at the beginning of Masoretic chapter 103, which is translated into Greek as tô Dauid (τῷ Δαυιδ) at the beginning of the Septuagint's chapter 102. This suggests that the replacements of the Aramaic word that meant "lord" were still not standard in the Hebrew translations during the Hasmonean Dynasty.

• Aleppo Codex: yhŭh mlk (יהוה מלך). Translation: yhŭh king

• Leningrad Codex: yehvah malach (יְהוָה מָלָךְ). Translation: Yehvah king

• Targum to Psalms: yeyā melāk (יְיָ מְלָךְ). Translation: Yah king

As this variation dates to after the Greek translation of Psalms, the direct translation of "the lord is the king" from the Greek is used.

Psalms: Chapter 99

A psalm for thanksgiving.

Make a joyful noise to the Lord, all the earth! Serve the Lord with gladness, and come before his presence with celebration. Know that the Lord is God. He made us, and not we ourselves. We are his people and the sheep of his pasture. Enter into his gates with thanksgiving, and his courts with hymns, and give thanks to him. Praise his name! The Lord is good, his mercy is forever, and his truth endures from generation to generation.

Psalms: Chapter 100

A psalm of David. I will sing to you, Lord, of mercy and judgment.

I will sing a psalm, and I will be wise in a blameless way. When will you come to me? I walked in the innocence of my heart, in my house. I have not set before my eyes any unlawful thing, and I have hated transgressors. A perverse heart has not clung to me, and I have not known an evil man, as he turns away from me. He who secretly speaks against his neighbor, I have driven from me. He who is proud of his looks and insatiable in his heart, I have not eaten with him. My eyes will be on the faithful of the land, so they may live with me, and he who followed the way perfectly, also served me. The proud did not live in my house, and the unjust speaker did not prosper in my sight. I killed all the sinners in the land quickly, so I might destroy out of the city of the Lord all who work iniquity.

Psalms: Chapter 101

A prayer for the poor, when he was deeply affected and poured out his supplication before the Lord.

Hear my prayer, Lord, and let my cry come to you. Don't turn away your face from me on the day when I am afflicted, hear me on the day when I will call on you, quickly listen to me. For my days have vanished like smoke, and my bones have been parched like a stick. I am blighted like grass, and my heart is dried up, for I have forgotten to eat my bread because of the voice of my moaning, my bone is clinging to my flesh. I have become like a pelican of the wilderness. I have become like an owl in a ruined house. I have watched, and have become like a sparrow living alone on a roof. All day long, my enemies have insulted me, and those who praised me have sworn against me.

I have eaten ash as it were bread, and mingled my drink with tears, because of your anger and your fury. For you have lifted me up and dashed me down. My days have declined like a shadow, and I am withered like grass. But you, Lord, endure forever, and your memorial to generation and generation. You will rise, and have mercy on Zion, for it is time to have mercy on her, for the set time has come. Your servants have taken pleasure in her stones, and they will pity her dust. The nations will fear your name, Lord, and all kings your glory.

The Lord will build up Zion and will appear in his glory. He has had regard to the prayer of the lowly and has not despised their petition. Let this be written for another generation, and the people that will be created will praise the Lord. For he has looked out from the height of his sanctuary, the Lord looked on the earth from the sky, to hear the groaning of the chained ones, to loosen the sons of the slain, to proclaim the name of the Lord in Zion, and his praise in Jerusalem, when the people are gathered together, and the kings, to serve the Lord.

He answered him in the way of his strength. Tell me how few are my days. Don't take me away in the middle of my days, and your years are through all generations. In the beginning, you, Lord, laid the foundation of the earth, and the sky is the works of your hands. They will perish, but you remain, and they all will grow old like a garment, and as clothing will you fold them, and they will be changed. But you are the same, and your years will not fail. The children of your servants will live securely, and their seed will be directed correctly forever.

Psalms: Chapter 102

A psalm of David.

Bless the Lord, my mind, and all that is within me, bless his holy name. Bless the Lord, my mind, and don't forget all his praises, who forgives all your transgressions, who heals all your diseases, who redeems your life from corruption, who crowns you with mercy and compassion, who satisfies your desire with good things, so that your youth will be renewed like that of the eagle. The Lord executes mercy and judgment for all who are injured. He made known his ways to Moses, and his will to the Israelites. The Lord is compassionate, pitiful, patient, and full of mercy.

He will not always be angry, and neither will he be wrathful forever. He has not dealt with us according to our sins, nor repaid us according to our iniquities. For as the sky is high above the earth, the Lord has so increased his mercy towards those who fear him. As far as the east is from the west, so far has he removed our transgressions from us. As a father pities his children, the Lord pities those who fear him. For he knows our frame and remembers that we are dust. As for man, his days are like the grass. Like a flower of the field, so will he flourish.

For the wind passes over it, and it will not be, and it will know its place no more. But the mercy of the Lord is from generation to generation on those who fear him, and his righteousness to children's children, to those who keep his covenant and remember his commandments to do them. The Lord has prepared his throne in the sky, and his kingdom rules over all. Bless the Lord, all you, his messengers, mighty in strength, who perform his bidding, ready to listen to the voice of his words. Bless the Lord, all you, his armies, you ministers of his that do his will. Bless the Lord, all his works, in every place of his dominion, and bless the Lord, my mind.

Psalms: Chapter 103

A Psalm of David.

Bless the Lord, my mind. Lord my god, you are very great. You have clothed yourself with praise and honor, who robes yourself with light as with a garment and spreads out the sky like a curtain. Who covers his chambers with water? Who makes the clouds his chariot? Who walks on the wings of the wind? Who makes his messenger spirits, and his ministers a flaming fire? Who establishes the earth on her certain foundation? It will not be moved forever.

The deep, as it were a garment, is his covering, and the waters will stand on the hills. At your rebuke, they will flee, and at the voice of your thunder, they will be alarmed. They go up to the mountains, and down to the plains, to the place which you have founded for them. You have set a boundary which they will not pass, neither will they turn again to cover the earth. He sends forth his fountains among the valleys, and the waters will run between the mountains.

They will give waters to all the wild beasts of the field, and the wild donkeys will take from them to quench their thirst. Through them the birds of the sky will live, and they will speak in their voice from among the rocks. He waters the mountains from his chambers, and the earth will be satisfied with the fruit of your works. He makes grass to grow for the livestock, and green plants for the service of men, to bring bread out of the earth. Wine makes the heart of man happy, oil makes his face cheerful, and bread strengthens man's heart.

The trees of the plain will be full of sap, even the cedars of Lebanon which he has planted. There the sparrows will build their nests, and the house of the heron takes the lead among them. The high mountains are a refuge for the stags and the rock for the rabbits. He appointed the moon for seasons, and the sun knows when he is going down. You made darkness, and it was night, and in it, all the wild beasts of the forest will roam, even young lions roaring for prey, seeking meat for themselves from God.

The sun rises, and they will be gathered together and will lie down in their dens. Man will go out to his work, and labor until evening. How great are your works, Lord! In wisdom have you worked them all, and the earth is filled with your creation. So is this great and wide sea, and there are things creeping innumerable, small animals and great.

The ships go there, and the dragon that you have made to play in it. All wait on you, to give them their food in due season. When you have given it to them, they will gather it, and when you have opened your hand, they will all be filled with good. But when you have turned away your face, they will be troubled, and you will take away their breath, and they will fail, and return to their dust.

You will send out your spirit, and they will be created, and you will renew the face of the earth. Let the glory of the Lord be forever. The Lord will rejoice in his works, and who looks on the earth, and makes it tremble, who touches the mountains, and they smoke. I will sing to the Lord while I live, and I will sing praise to my god while I exist. Let my meditation be sweet to him, and I will rejoice in the Lord. Let the sinners fail from off the earth, and transgressors so that they will be no more. Bless the Lord, my mind.

Psalms: Chapter 104

Alleluia!

Give thanks to the Lord, and call on his name! Declare his works among the tribes. Sing to him, yes, sing praises to him! Tell all his wonderful works. Glory in his holy name! Let the heart of those who seek the Lord rejoice. Seek the Lord, and be strengthened. Seek his face continually. Remember the wonderful works that he did and his wonders, and the judgments of his mouth you descendants of Abram, his servants, you children of Jacob, his chosen ones.

He is the Lord our god, and his judgments are on all the earth. He has remembered his covenant forever, the word which he commanded for a thousand generations, which he established as a covenant to Abram, and he remembered his oath to Isaac. He established it to Jacob for an ordinance, and to Israel for an eternal covenant, saying, "I will give you the land of Canaan, to the line of your descendants," when they were few in number, very few, and foreigners in it.

They went from nation to nation, and from one kingdom to another people. He allowed no man to wrong them, and he rebuked kings for their sake, saying, "Don't touch my anointed ones, and don't harm my prophets." Moreover, he called for a famine on the land, and he broke the whole support of bread.

He sent a man before them, Joseph who was sold as a slave. They humbled his feet with shackles, his body was held in iron until the time that his cause appeared, and the word of the Lord tested him like fire. The king sent and released him, the prince of the people, and let him go free. He made him lord over his house, and ruler of all his property, to chastise his rulers at his pleasure, and to teach his elders wisdom.

Israel also came into Egypt, and Jacob stayed in the land of Ham. He increased his people greatly and made them stronger than their enemies. He turned their heart to hate his people, to deal craftily with his servants. He sent out Moses his servant and Aaron whom he had chosen. He established among them his signs and his wonders in the land of Ham. He sent out darkness and made it dark, yet they ignored his words.

He turned their waters into blood and killed their fish. Their land produced frogs abundantly, in the chambers of their kings. He spoke, and the dog-fly came, and lice within all their frontiers. He turned their rain into hail and sent flaming fire into their land. He struck their vines and their fig trees and broke every tree within their frontiers. He spoke, and the locust came, and uncountable caterpillars devoured all the grass in their land, and devoured the fruit of the land. He struck also every firstborn of their land, the first fruits of all their labor. He brought them out with silver and gold, and there was not a feeble one among their tribes. Egypt rejoiced at their departing, as they had come to fear them.

He spread out a cloud for a cover over them, and fire to give them light by night. They asked, and the quail came, and he satisfied them with the bread of the sky. He cleaved the rock, and the waters flowed, and rivers ran in dry places. For he remembered his holy word, which he promised to Abraham his servant. He brought out his people with celebration, and his chosen with joy and gave them the lands of the peoples, and they inherited the labors of the people, that they might keep his ordinances, and diligently seek his law.

Psalms: Chapter 105

Alleluia!

Give thanks to the Lord, for he is good, and his mercy endures forever. Who will tell the mighty acts of the Lord? Who will cause all his praises to be heard? Blessed are those who keep judgment, and do righteousness at all times. Remember us, Lord, with the favor you have to your people. Visit us with your salvation, that we may see the good of your choice, that we may rejoice in the celebration of your nation, and that we may glory with your inheritance.

We have sinned with our fathers, we have transgressed, we have done unrighteously. Our fathers in Egypt did not understand your wonders and did not remember the multitude of your mercy, yet provoked you as they went up by the Papyrus Sea.[1] Yet he saved them for his name's sake, that he might cause his mighty power to be known. He rebuked the Papyrus Sea, and it was dried up, and he led them through the deep as through the wilderness. He saved them out of the hands of those who hated them and redeemed them out of the hands of the enemy.

The waters covered those who oppressed them, and there was none of them left. Then they believed his words and celebrated his praise. They quickly forgot his works, and they did not wait for his counsel. They lusted greatly in the wilderness and tempted God in the desert. He gave them their request and sent fullness into their minds. They provoked Moses also in the camp, and Aaron the holy one of the Lord. The earth opened and swallowed up Dathan, and closed on the congregation of Abiram. A fire was started in their congregation, and a flame burnt up the sinners.

They made a calf in Horeb and worshiped the carved image, and they changed their glory into the image of a calf that feeds on grass. They forgot the god who saved them, who had worked great deeds in Egypt, wondrous works in the land of Ham, and terrible things at the Papyrus Sea. So he said that he would have destroyed them, had not Moses his chosen stood before him in the breach, to turn him away from the fierceness of his anger, so that he should not destroy them.

Moreover, they set at nothing the desirable land and did not believe his word. They murmured in their tents, and they did not listen to the voice of the Lord. So he lifted his hand against them, to throw them down in the wilderness, and to throw down their seed among the nations, and to scatter them in the lands. They were joined also to Ba'al Peor and ate the sacrificed dead. They provoked him with their plans, and destruction was multiplied among them.

Then Phinehas stood up and made atonement, and the plague ceased. It was counted to him for righteousness, to all generations forever. They provoked him also at the water of strife, and Moses was hurt for their sake, for they provoked his spirit, and he commanded unadvisedly with his lips. They did not destroy the nations which the Lord commanded them to destroy, but were mixed with the nations, and learned their works. They served their engraved images, and it became an offense to them.

They sacrificed their sons and their daughters to demons,[2] and shed innocent blood, the blood of their sons and daughters, whom they sacrificed to the idols of Canaan, and the land was murderously defiled with blood and was polluted with their works, and they went a whoring with their own plans. So the Lord was very angry with his people, and he abhorred his inheritance. He delivered them into the hands of their enemies, and those who hated them ruled over them, and their enemies oppressed them, and they were brought down under their hands.

He saved them many times, but they provoked him by their counsel, and they were brought low by their iniquities. You, Lord, saw their affliction when he heard their petition. He remembered his covenant and repented according to the multitude of his mercy. He caused them to be pitied in the sight of all who carried them captive. Save us, Lord our god, and gather us from among the foreigners, that we may give thanks to your holy name, that we may glory in your praise. Blessed is Lord the god of Israel from forever and for all eternity, and all the people will say, "Amen, Amen."[3]

Psalms: Chapter 105 Notes

1 Codex Vacticanus: erythra thalassê (𝒆𝒓𝒚𝒆𝒑𝒂𝒆𝒂𝒍𝒍𝒂𝒄𝒄𝒉) Translation: Erythra Sea

• Aleppo Codex: ym-sŭp (םי־ףוס). Translation: Sea of Papyrus

• Leningrad Codex: yam-sûp (יַם־סוּף). Translation: Sea of Papyrus

• Targum to Psalms: yamā desûp (יְמָא דְסוּף). Translation: sea of reeds

The Greek term is not geographically specific, allowing for the Israelites to have passed from Egypt to the wilderness at any point in the Red Sea or even the Gulf of Aden. The Greek name appears to be a translation of the Persian term Erostras, which referred to the entire Persian Gulf, Red Sea, and the Indian Ocean. The Greeks were likely referring to the Gulf of Suez, however, this was known to the ancient Egyptians as the "Sea of Calm," which is what the Israelites would have called it if that was where they were.

The Greeks transliterated the name as the Sea of Siph (θαλάσσησ Σιφ) in the Codex Vaticanus' translation of Judges, confirming that the name Sûf was in the Aramaic text they worked from. The Aramaic term sûf (סוף) and Phoenician term sûf (𐤑𐤅𐤐), both meaning papyrus plants were adopted from the Egyptian term tjûfî (𓆱𓆷𓈖𓏏), which referred to papyrus, papyrus plants, and papyrus marshes. The Egyptian term continued to be used into the Classical era as the Coptic words čoouf (ϫⲟⲟⲩϥ), conf (ϭⲟⲛϥ), and comf (ϭⲟⲙϥ), all meaning papyrus. Conversely, the Egyptian name of the Red Sea was the Sea of Ḥeh (𓎛), meaning "very large sea" from the Middle Kingdom era onward, however, believed to have originally been named after the ancient Egyptian frog god Ḥeh (𓁗). As the Greek translation of Erythrean Sea is anachronistic, the translation of Papyrus Sea is imported from the Masoretic text.

2 Codex Vacticanus: daemonioes (ⲆⲀⲓⲘⲞⲚⲓⲞⲓⲥ).
Translation: divinities (or lesser gods)

- Aleppo Codex: šdym (שדים). Translation: demons
- Leningrad Codex: shedim (שֵׁדִים). Translation: demons
- Targum to Psalms: mazîqayā (מְזִיקַיָּא). Translation: demons

3 Codex Vacticanus: genoeto genoeto (ⲄⲉⲚⲞⲓⲦⲞ ⲄⲉⲚⲞⲓⲦⲞ). Translation: Earth forbid, Earth forbid

- Aleppo Codex: åmn hllû-yh (אמן הללו-יה). Translation: Amn praise Yah
- Leningrad Codex: amen hallu-yah (אָמֵן הַלְלוּ-יָהּ). Translation: Amen praise Yah

• Targum to Psalms: āmēn hallûyāh (אָמֵן הַלְלוּיָה). Translation: Amen praise Yah

The Greeks translated the Aramaic word åmyn (אֵלֵל) as
"Earth forbid" (γένοιτο) when translating the Septuagint. As
the Aramaic text could not have included the Greek
expression, the term Amen is used in this translation.

Psalms: Chapter 106

Alleluia!

Give thanks to the Lord, for he is good, and his mercy endures forever. Let them say so, those who have been redeemed by the Lord, he who has redeemed from the hand of the enemy, and gathered them out of the countries, from the east, and west, and north, and sea. They wandered in the wilderness, in a desert they found no road to an inhabited city. Hungry and thirsty, their mind fainted within them. Then they cried to the Lord in their affliction, and he delivered them out of their distresses. He guided them along a straight path so they might go to an inhabited city.

Let them acknowledge the Lord's mercies and his wonderful works for the children of men.

For he satisfies the empty mind and fills the hungry mind with good things, even those who sit in darkness and the shadow of death, fettered in poverty and iron, because they rejected the oracles, and provoked the counsel of the Highest. Their heart was brought low with troubles, and they were weak, and there was no helper. Then they cried to the Lord in their affliction, and he saved them out of their distresses. He brought them out of the darkness and the shadow of death and broke their bonds asunder.

Let them acknowledge the Lord's mercies and his wonderful works for the children of men.

He broke to pieces the bronze gates and crushed the iron bars. He helped them out of their iniquity, for they were brought low because of their iniquities. Their mind abhorred all food, and they approached the gates of death. Then they cried to the Lord in their affliction, and he saved them out of their distresses. He sent his word and healed them, and delivered them out of their destruction.

Let them acknowledge the Lord's mercies and his wonderful works for the children of men.

Let them offer to him the sacrifice of praise, and proclaim this work with celebration. Those who go down to the sea in ships, doing business in many waters. These men have seen the works of the Lord, and his wonders in the deep. He speaks, and the stormy wind arises, and its waves are lifted. They go up to the sky and go down to the depths, and their mind melts because of troubles. They are troubled, they stagger like a drunkard, and all their wisdom is swallowed up. Then they cry to the Lord in their affliction, and he brings them out of their distresses. He commands the storm, and it is calmed into a gentle breeze, and its waves are still.

They are glad because they are quiet, and he guides them to their desired haven.

Let them acknowledge the Lord's mercies and his wonderful works for the children of men.

Let them praise him in the congregation of the people, and praise him in the seat of the elders. He turns rivers into a desert, and streams of water into a wasteland, a fruitful land into saltiness, because of the iniquity of those who live in it. He turns a wilderness into pools of water and a desert into streams of water. There he causes the hungry to live, and they establish for themselves cities to inhabit. They sow fields and plant vineyards, and they yield increasing fruits. He blesses them, and they greatly multiply, and he does not diminish the number of their livestock. Again they became few and were brought low by the pressure of evils and pains. Contempt is poured on their princes, and he causes them to wander in a desert and trackless land. But he helps the poor out of poverty and makes his family like a flock. The upright will see and rejoice, and all iniquity will stop her mouth. Who is wise, and will observe these things, and understand the mercies of the Lord?

Psalms: Chapter 106 Notes

1 Codex Vacticanus: logon (ⲗⲟⲅⲟⲛ) Translation: his word (or sentence, utterance)

• Aleppo Codex: dbrǔ (דכרו). Translation: his voice (or leader, plague, pestilence)

• Leningrad Codex: devaro (דְּבָרוֹ). Translation: his voice (or leader, plague, pestilence)

• Targum to Psalms: pitgāmê (פִּתְגָמֵי). Translation: proverb (or writ, saying)

The voice of God was a major spirit and said to be his original creation in the Spoken Orit which was quoted in Ge'ez 1ˢᵗ Maccabees. This parallels the Egyptian belief that Atum, the creator, spoke the first word: hǔ (𓀀𓏞), when he created the world. However, the Voice in Ge'ez 1ˢᵗ Maccabees was feminine and appears to be another name for the Hand of God, which is mentioned repeatedly in the Torah, Psalms, and the Solomonic literature. In the creation mythology of Ỉůnů (Aůn, Heliopolis), Atum created the world with his wife Iusaaset, who was described as the "Hand of Atum." Like Asherah in Jerusalem, she was associated with self-pollinating "virgin" trees, and like Shalim, the god Jerusalam and King Solomon were named after, her husband Atum was associated with the evening.

An alternate interpretation of hǔ (𓀀𓏞) was found in the cult of Ptah, a rival creator god the Egyptians adopted from the Minoan civilization. In the cult of Ptah, Hů was the word that Ptah spoke that created the world, Ptah had no wife.

322

This concept of Hū appears to have influenced the development of the Gnostic-Christian Gospel of John, which begins with the statement, "In the beginning was the Word, and the Word was with God, and the Word was God."

Ptah continued to be worshipped in the Middle East, until at least the development of Mandaeism, as he became the Mandaean angel Ptahil (ܠܝܚܐܬܦ).The origin of the Mandaeans is not clear, however, they were present in the Parthian empire before 224 AD, where they flourished. Their belief regarding their history is that they are the descendants of the followers of John the Baptist who did not follow Jesus after John was executed. Before the time of John, their sect had followed the teachings of the patriarchs, Adam, Abel, Seth, Enos, Noah, Shem, and Aram, but not Abraham, Moses, or the other Israelite and Judean prophets. The sect likely developed in Syria under Assyrian, Babylonian, or Persian rule.

In the third century AD, the prophet Mani, the founder of Manichaeism, radically reinterpreted Ptahil as the Prince of Darkness, who invaded the world of light leading to the creation of the universe. In some respects, this parallels the older Solomonic belief that Mot (death) invaded the world of the living because he was jealous of God's love of humans.

Based on the remnants of the Spoken Orit, it is most likely that the Aramaic source texts the Greeks used would have used the word dbr (רבד) like the Hebrew translation, which the Greeks interpreted as "word," but would have been interpreted as "voice," by the Aramaic speaking Judeans. However, the older Canaanite meaning of dbr (𐤃𐤁𐤓), meaning "plague," makes more sense in the verse. If that was the original meaning, the verse would have read: "He sent his plague but healed them, and delivered them out of their destruction."

Psalms: Chapter 107

Song of a Psalm by David.

God, my heart is ready, my heart is ready, and I will sing and sing psalms with my glory. Awake, lute and harp! I will wake up early! I will give thanks to you, Lord, among the people, and I will sing praise to you among the nations. For your mercy is great above Shamayim, and your truth reaches to the clouds. Be praised god above Shamayim, and your glory is above the whole earth. So your beloved ones may be delivered, save with your right hand, and hear me. God has spoken in his sanctuary, and I will be praised, and will divide Shechem, and will measure out the valley of tents.

Gilead is mine!

Manasseh is mine!

Ephraim helps my head!

Judah is my king!

Moab is the cauldron of my hope!

Over Edom, I will tread in my sandals, and the Pelesets are made subject to me.

Who will bring me into the fortified city? Who will guide me to Edom? Won't you, God who has rejected us? Will not you, God, go out with our armies? Give us help from tribulation, for vain is the help of man.

Through God, we will work powerfully, and he will bring to nothing our enemies.

Psalms: Chapter 108

A Psalm of David.

God, don't ignore my praise in silence, for the mouth of the sinner and the mouth of the cunning man have been opened against me. They have spoken against me with a cunning tongue. They have surrounded me with words of hatred and fought against me without a cause. In return for my love, they falsely accused me, but I continued to pray. They rewarded me evil for good, and hatred for my love. You set a sinner against him and let the accuser stand at his right hand.

When he is judged, let him go out condemned, and let his prayer become sin. Let his days be few, and let another take his office of overseer. Let his children be orphans, and his wife a widow. Let his children wander without a home, and beg, and let them be thrown out of their habitations. Let his creditor exact all that belongs to him, and let strangers spoil his labors. Let him have no helper, nor let anyone have compassion on his fatherless children. Let his children be given up to destruction, and in one generation let his name be blotted out.

Let the iniquity of his fathers be remembered before the Lord, and don't let the sin of his mother be blotted out. Let them remain before the Lord continually, and let their memory be blotted out from the earth. Because he did not remember to show mercy, but persecuted the needy and poor man, and killed him by stabbing him in the heart. He loved cursing also, and so it will come on him, and he took no pleasure in blessing, so it will be removed far from him.

Yes, he put on cursing like a garment, and it has come as water into his bowels, and like oil into his bones. Let it be for him as a garment which he puts on, and as a girdle with which he girds himself continually. This is the dealing of the Lord with those who falsely accuse me, and of those who speak evil against my mind. But you, Lord my Lord,[1] deal mercifully with me, for your name's sake, and your mercy is good. Deliver me, for I am poor and needy, and my heart is troubled within me. I am removed like a shadow in its going down, and I am tossed up and down like locusts. My knees are weakened through fasting, and my flesh is changed because of the lack of oil. I became also a reproach to them, and when they saw me they shook their heads.

Help me, Lord my god, and save me according to your mercy. Let them know that this is your hand and that you, Lord, have worked it. Let them curse, but you will bless, and let those who rise up against me be ashamed, but let your servant rejoice. Let those who falsely accuse me be clothed with shame, and let them cover themselves with their shame as with a mantle. I will give thanks to the Lord abundantly with my mouth, and in the middle of many, I will praise him. For he stood on the right hand of the poor, to save me from those who persecuted my mind.

Psalms: Chapter 108 Notes

1 Codex Vacticanus: cyrie cyrie (ΚΥΡΙΕΚΥΡΙΕ). Translation: lord lord

• Aleppo Codex: yhŭh ådny (יהוה אדני). Translation: Yhŭh my lord

• Leningrad Codex: yehvih adonai (יְהוִה אֲדֹנָי). Translation: Yehvih my lord

• Targum to Psalms: ĕlōhîm yeyā (אֱלֹהִים יְיָ). Translation: gods Yah

As the Greeks translated Yhŭ (יהו) as Iaw (Ιαω) in some of the books of the Septuagint, however, there is no evidence that the Septuagint's book of Psalms ever included the name Iaw. This expression of "lord lord" (κύριε κύριε) could only have been translated from the Aramaic term bôlå ådny (בולא אלעי).

Psalms: Chapter 109

A Psalm of David.

The Lord said to my lord, "Sit on my right hand until I make your enemies your footstool."

The Lord will send out his wand of power for you out of Zion and rule among your enemies. With you is dominion in the day of your power, in the splendors of your holiness. I have begotten you from the womb before the morning.

The Lord swore, and will not repent, "You are a priest forever, in the order of Melchizedek. The Lord at your right hand has dashed to pieces kings in the day of his anger. He will judge among the nations. He will fill up with the number of corpses, and he will crush the heads of many on the earth. He will drink of the brook along the way, and therefore will he lift up his head."

Psalms: Chapter 110

Alleluia!

I will thank you, Lord, with my whole heart, in the council of the upright, and in the congregation. The works of the Lord are great, worked out according to all his will. His work is worthy of thanksgiving and honor, and his righteousness endures forever and ever.

He has caused his wonderful works to be remembered. The Lord is merciful and compassionate. He has given food to those who fear him. He will remember his covenant forever. He has declared to his people the power of his works, to give them the inheritance of the nations. The works of his hands are truth and judgment.

All his commandments are sure, and established forever and ever, done in truth and uprightness. He sent redemption to his people, and he commanded his covenant forever. Holy and fearsome is his name. The fear of the Lord is the sum of wisdom, and all that comprehend it, follow it. His praise endures forever and ever.

Psalms: Chapter 111

Alleluia!

Blessed is the man that fears the Lord, and he will delight greatly in his commandments. His seed will be mighty in the earth, and the generation of the upright will be blessed. Glory and riches will be in his house, and his righteousness endures forever.

To the upright light has sprung up in darkness, and he is pitiful and merciful, and righteous. The good man is he who pities and lends, and he will direct his affairs with justice. For he will not be moved forever, and the righteous will be remembered forever. He will not be afraid of any evil report, and his heart is ready to trust in the Lord. His heart is established, he will not fear, till he sees his desire against his enemies.

He has dispersed abroad, and he has given to the poor, and his righteousness endures forever. His radiance[1] will be praised with honor. The sinner will see and be angry, he will gnash his teeth, and consume away, and the desire of the sinner will perish.

Psalms: Chapter 111 Notes

1 Codex Vacticanus: ceras (ⲕⲉⲣⲁⲥ). Translation: horn (or arm)

- Aleppo Codex: qrnů (קרנו). Translation: horn (or radiance, power)
- Leningrad Codex: karno (קַרְנוֹ). Translation: horn (or radiance, power)
- Targum to Psalms: tûqepêh (תּוּקְפֵיה). Translation: validity

The reference is generally assumed to refer to the horns on the altars in ancient Canaan. An alternate belief among early Christians until the Middle Ages was that the Lord had horns. Yhůh was depicted as having horns in the earliest depictions of him found at Kuntillet Ajrud in the Sinai desert from the 9th century BC, so clearly, the early Israelites did believe Yhůh had horns. The title Ba'al Qarnim (𐤏𐤋 𐤒𐤓𐤍𐤌), meaning Lord Horns, was applied to the Canaanite god Hammon during this era. Lord Hammon was also described as being a solar and fertility god, and the king of the gods, like the god in most of the Psalms, suggesting that before the Yahwist redactor, the Psalms were about Lord Hammon.

Psalms: Chapter 112

Alleluia!

Praise the Lord, you servants of his! Praise the name of the Lord. Let the name of the Lord be blessed from now and forever. From the rising of the sun to his setting, the name of the Lord is to be praised. The Lord is high above all the nations, and his glory is above Shamayim. Who is like the Lord our god? Who lives in the high place, and yet looks on the low things in the sky and the earth? Who lifts the poor from the earth, and raises the needy from the dunghill to set him with princes, even with the princes of his people? Who settles the barren woman in a house, as a mother rejoicing over children.

Psalms: Chapter 113

Alleluia!

When Israel left Egypt, the house of Jacob departed a barbarous people, and Judah became his sanctuary, and Israel his dominion. The sea saw it and fled, and the Jordan was turned back. The Mountains ran like rams, and the hills like lambs. What about you, Yam, who fled, and you Jordan, who turned back? You mountains, that you skipped like rams, and you hills, like lambs? Eretz trembled at the presence of the Lord, at the presence of the god of Jacob, who turned the rock into pools of water, and the flint into fountains of water.

Psalms: Chapter 114

Not for us, Lord, not for us, but for your name give glory, because of your mercy and your truth, in case at any time the nations should say, "Where is their God?"

Our God has done whatever he has pleased in the sky and on earth. The idols of the nations are silver and gold, the works of men's hands. They have a mouth, but they will not speak. They have eyes, but they will not see. They have ears, but they will not hear. They have noses, but they will not smell. They have hands, but they will not handle anything. They have feet, but they will not walk. They will not speak through their throat. Let those who make them become like them and all who trust in them.

The house of Israel trusts in the Lord, for he is their helper and defender. The house of Aaron trusts in the Lord, and he is their helper and defender. They who fear the Lord trust in the Lord, as he is their helper and defender. The Lord has remembered us and blessed us. He has blessed the house of Israel, he has blessed the house of Aaron. He has blessed those who fear the Lord, both small and great. The Lord increases you and your children. Blessed are you by the Lord, who made the sky and the earth. The sky above Shamayim belongs to the Lord, but he has given the earth to the sons of Adam. The dead will not praise you, Lord, nor any that go down to Sheol. But we, the living, will bless the Lord, from now on and forever.

Psalms: Chapter 115

Alleluia!

I am very happy because the Lord will listen to the voice of my supplication. Because he has turned his ear to me, I will call on him as long as I live. The pangs of Mot surround me, and the dangers of Sheol have found me. I found affliction and sorrow.

Then I called on the name of the Lord, "Lord, deliver my mind!" and the Lord is merciful and righteous. Yes, our god has pity. The Lord saves the infants. I was humbled, yet he delivered me. Return to your rest, my mind, for the Lord has dealt bountifully with you. For he has delivered my mind from death, my eyes from tears, and my feet from falling. I will be well-pleasing before the Lord in the land of the living.

Alleluia!

I believed, therefore I have spoken, but I was greatly afflicted. I said in my amazement, "Every man is a liar."

What will I give to the Lord for all the things in which he has rewarded me? I will take the cup of salvation, and call on the name of the Lord. I will pay my vows to the Lord, in the presence of all his people. Precious in the sight of the Lord is the death of his sacred. Lord, I am your servant. I am your servant and the son of your handmaid. You have burst my bonds asunder. I will offer to you the sacrifice of praise and will call on the name of the Lord. I will pay my vows to the Lord, in the presence of all his people, in the courts of the Lord's temple, in the middle of you, Jerusalem.

Psalms: Chapter 116

Alleluia!

Praise the Lord, all you nations! Praise him, all you peoples! For his mercy has been abundant towards us, and the truth of the Lord endures forever.

Psalms: Chapter 117

Alleluia!

Give thanks to the Lord as he is good, for his mercy endures forever. Now let the house of Israel say that he is good, for his mercy endures forever. Let now the house of Aaron say, that he is good, for his mercy endures forever. Let all that fear the Lord say, that he is good, for his mercy endures forever. I called on the Lord out of affliction, and he listened to me, to bring me into a wide place. The Lord is my helper, and I will not fear what man will do to me. The Lord is my helper, and I will see my desire against my enemies. It is better to trust in the Lord than to trust in man. It is better to hope in the Lord than to hope in princes.

All nations surrounded me, but in the name of the Lord, I repulsed them. They surrounded me, but in the name of the Lord, I repulsed them. They surrounded me like bees surround a honeycomb, and they burst into flame as fire among thorns, but in the name of the Lord, I repulsed them. I was knocked and greatly shaken so I might fall, but the Lord helped me. The Lord is my strength and my song has become my salvation. The voice of celebration and salvation is in the tabernacles of Sydyk, and the right hand of the Lord has worked mightily. The right hand of the Lord has praised me, and the right hand of the Lord has worked powerfully.

I will not die, but live, and recount the works of the Lord. The Lord has punished me greatly, but he has not given me up to death. Open to me the gates of Sydyk,[1] and I will go into them, and give praise to the Lord. This is the gate of the Lord, and the righteous will enter by it. I will give thanks to you, because you have heard me, and have become my salvation. The stone which the builders rejected, became the cornerstone.

This has been done through the Lord, and it is wonderful in our eyes. This is the day that the Lord has made. Let us celebrate and rejoice in it. Lord, save me now! Lord,[2] send me prosperity now! Blessed is he that comes in the name of the Lord! We have blessed you out of the temple of the Lord. The Lord is God, and he has shined on us! Celebrate the feast with many branches, binding the victims to the horns of the altar.

You are my god, and I will give you thanks. You are my god, and I will praise you. I will give thanks to you, for you have heard me, and are become my salvation. Give thanks to the Lord, for he is good, and his mercy endures forever.

Psalms: Chapter 117 Notes

1 Codex Vacticanus: pylas dicaeosynês (ΠΥΛΑC ΔΙΚΑΙΟCΥΝΗC). Translation: gates of justice

- Dead Sea Scroll 4QPs^b: šôry sdq (צדק שׁערי). Translation: gateway of justice (or Sydyk)
- Aleppo Codex: šôry-ṣdq (שׁערי-צדק). Translation: gateway of justice (or Sydyk)
- Leningrad Codex: sha'arei-tzedek (שַׁעֲרֵי־צֶדֶק). Translation: gateway of justice (or Sydyk)
- Targum to Psalms: qartā dèṣidqā (קַרְתָּא דְצִדְקָא). Translation: city of justice

Sdq (𐤑𐤃𐤒)was the ancient Canaanite god of correctness, and brother of the god Mṣr (𐤌𐤔𐤓), the god of straightness. The primary source for information on these gods was the Bronze Age writer Sanchuniathon, whose surviving work was collected and translated into Greek by Philo of Byblos in the early 2nd century AD. Philo spelled the names as Sydyk (Συδυκ) and Misôr (Μισωρ), from which the English names are derived. Philo claimed they were the sons of the god Amônos (Αμωνος), which indicates that Sanchuniathon's text originally referred to the Canaanite god Ba'al Hmn (𐤁𐤏𐤋 𐤇𐤌𐤍), usually anglicized as Lord Hammon. Lord Hammon was the Canaanite equivalent of the North Egyptian Atum, South Egyptian Amen (𓇋𓏠𓈖), and Kushite Amanai (𓁦𓈖𓎡𓇋). Like Amen, Hammon was viewed as a solar deity, a fertility god, and the king of the gods. He was also associated with infant sacrifice, suggesting he was the god "Moloch" (king) that was banned under the rule of Josiah, when Yahwism was adopted, suggesting some of the original Psalms were about Hammon.

2 Codex Vacticanus: cyrie (ΚΥΡΙЄ). Translation: sir, lord

- The Great Psalms Scroll: yhůh (𐤉𐤄𐤅𐤆). 11QPsᵃ is a Hebrew language scroll with Yhůh written in the Canaanite script, proving that the name was being substituted into the text during the Herodian Dynasty.
- Aleppo Codex: yhůh (יהוה)
- Leningrad Codex: yehvah (יְהֹוָה)
- Targum to Psalms: yeyā (יי)

As there is no evidence of Yhůh being in Psalms before the Hasmoneans' Hebrew translation, the direct translation of Lord from cyrie (κύριε) is used.

Psalms: Chapter 118

Alleluia.

Blessed are the blameless who follow the law of the Lord. Blessed are those who search out his testimonies. They will diligently seek him with their whole heart. For those who work iniquity have not walked in his ways. You have commanded us diligently to keep your precepts. If only my ways were directed to keep your ordinances. Then I will not be ashamed when I have respect for all your commandments. I will give you thanks with uprightness of heart when I have learned the judgments of your righteousness.

I will keep your ordinances. Don't forget me. Where will a young man direct his way? By remembering your words. With my whole heart have I diligently trusted you, don't throw me away from your commandments. I have hidden your oracles in my heart, that I might not sin against you. Blessed are you, Lord, teach me your ordinances. With my lips, I have declared all the judgments of your mouth. I have delighted in the way of your testimonies, as much as in all riches.

I will meditate on your commandments, and consider your ways. I will meditate on your ordinances, and I will not forget your words. Repay your servant, so will I live, and keep your words. Unveil my eyes, and I will perceive wondrous things of your law. I am an alien on

Earth. Don't hide your commandments from me. My mind has longed exceedingly for your judgments at all times. You have rebuked the proud, and cursed are they who turn aside from your commandments.

Remove from me reproach and contempt, for I have searched through your testimonies. For princes sat and spoke against me, but your servant was meditating on your ordinances. For your testimonies are my meditation, and your ordinances are my counselors. My mind has clung to the ground, quicken you me according to your word. I declared my ways, and you heard me. Teach me your ordinances. Instruct me in the way of your ordinances, and I will meditate on your wondrous works.

My mind has slumbered for sorrow, strengthen me with your words. Remove from me the ways of iniquity, and be merciful to me in teaching me your law. I have chosen the way of truth, and have not forgotten your judgments. I have clung to your testimonies, Lord, don't put me to shame. I studied your commandments when you did enlarge my heart. Teach me, Lord, the way of your ordinances, and I will seek it out continually.

Instruct me, and I will study your law and will keep it with my whole heart. Guide me in the path of your commandments, for I have delighted in it. Incline my heart to your testimonies, and not to covetousness. Turn away my eyes so that I may not look vanity. Quicken me in your way. Confirm your oracle to your servant, that he may fear you. Take away my reproach, for your judgments are good. Look, I have desired your commandments. Quicken me in your righteousness. Let your mercy come on me, Lord,[1] even your salvation, according to your word. So I will be able to answer those who insult me, for I have trusted in your words.

Don't take the word of truth completely out of my mouth, for I have trusted in your judgments. So I will keep your law continually, forever and ever. I also wandered widely, for I studied your commandments. I spoke of your testimonies before kings and was not ashamed. I studied your commandments, which I loved greatly. I lifted my hands to your commandments which I loved, and I meditated in your ordinances. Remember your words to your servant, in which you have made me hope. This has comforted me in my affliction, for your oracle has quickened me. The proud have transgressed greatly, but I did not deviate from your law.

I remembered your judgments of old, Lord, and was comforted. Despair took hold of me, because of the sinners who forget your law. Your ordinances were my songs in the place of my traveling. I remembered your name, Lord, in the night, and kept your law. This I had because I diligently studied your ordinances. You are my portion, Lord. I said that I would keep your law. I implored your presence with my whole heart, and have mercy on me according to your word. I thought of your ways and turned my feet to your testimonies. I prepared myself, (and was not terrified,) to keep your commandments. The snares of sinners entangled me, but I did not forget your law.

At midnight I arose, to give thanks to you for the judgments of your righteousness. I am a companion of all those who fear you, and of those who keep your commandments. Lord, the earth is full of your mercy, and teach me your ordinances. You have worked kindly with your servant, Lord, according to your word. Teach me kindness, and instruction, and knowledge, for I have believed your commandments. Before I was afflicted, I transgressed, and therefore I have followed your word. You are good, Lord, therefore in your goodness teach me your ordinances. The injustice of the proud has been multiplied against me, but I will follow your commandments with all my heart.

Their heart has been curdled like milk, but I have meditated on your law. It is good for me that you have afflicted me, and that I might learn your ordinances. The law of your mouth is better to me than thousands of gold and silver. Your hands have made me, and fashioned me, and instruct me, that I may learn your commandments. They who fear you will see me and rejoice, for I have trusted in your words. I know, Lord, that your judgments are righteous, and that you in truthfulness have afflicted me.

I beg you, let your mercy be a comfort to me, according to your word to your servant. Let your compassion come to me, that I may live, for your law is my concern. Let the proud be ashamed, for they transgressed against me unjustly, but I will meditate in your commandments. Let those who fear you, and those who know your testimonies, turn to me. Let my heart be blameless in your ordinances, that I may not be ashamed. My mind faints for your salvation, and I have trusted in your words. My eyes failed in waiting for your word, saying, "When will you comfort me? For I have become like a bottle in the frost," yet I have not forgotten your ordinances.

How many are the days of your servant? When will you execute judgment for me on those who persecute me? Transgressors told me idle tales, but not according to your law, Lord. All your commandments are truth, and they persecuted me unjustly. Help me! They nearly made an end of me on the earth, but I did not forget your commandments. Quicken me according to your mercy, so I will keep the testimonies of your mouth.

Your word, Lord, lives in the sky forever. Your truth endures for all generations. You have founded the earth, and it lives. The day continues by your plan, for all things are your servants. Was it not your law that is my meditation? Should I have perished in my affliction? I will never forget your ordinances, for with them you have quickened me.

I am yours, save me, for I have studied your ordinances. Sinners laid wait for me to destroy me, but I understood your testimonies. I have seen an end of all perfection, but your commandment is very broad. How I have loved your law, Lord! I meditate on it all day. You have made me wiser than my enemies in your commandment, for it is mine forever. I have more understanding than all my teachers, for your testimonies are my medication. I understand more than the aged because I have studied your commandments. I have held back my feet from every evil path, that I might keep your words. I have not declined from your judgments, for you have instructed me.

How sweet are your oracles to my throat! More so than honey to my mouth! I gain understanding by your commandments, therefore I have hated every way of unrighteousness. Your law is a lamp to my feet and a light to my paths. I have sworn and am determined to keep the judgments of your righteousness. I have been very greatly afflicted, Lord. Quicken me, according to your word. I beg you, Lord, accept the free will offerings of my mouth and teach me your judgments. My mind is continually in your hands, and I have not forgotten your law. Sinners spread a snare for me, but I did not err from your commandments. I have inherited your testimonies forever, for they are the joy of my heart.

I have inclined my heart to perform your ordinances forever, in return for your mercies. I have hated transgressors, but I have loved your law. You are my helper and my supporter, and I have trusted in your words. Leave from me, you evil-doers, for I will study the commandments of my god. Uphold me according to your word, and quicken me. Don't make me ashamed of my expectations. Help me, and I will be saved, and I will meditate in your ordinances continually. You have brought to nothing all that leave from your ordinances, for their inward thought is unrighteous. I have reckoned all the sinners of the earth as transgressors, therefore I have loved your testimonies.

Penetrate my flesh with your fear, for I am afraid of your judgments. I have done judgment and justice, so don't deliver me up to those who injure me. Receive your servant for good, and don't let the proud accuse me falsely. My eyes have searched your salvation and for the word of your righteousness. Deal with your servant according to your mercy, and teach me your ordinances. I am your servant, instruct me, and I will know your testimonies.

It is time for the Lord to work! They have completely broken your law, while have I loved your commandments more than gold or topaz. Therefore I directed myself according to all your commandments, and I have hated every unjust way. Your testimonies are wonderful, and therefore my mind has searched them out. The manifestation of your words will enlighten, and instruct the simple. I opened my mouth, and drew breath, for I earnestly longed after your commandments. Look on me and have mercy on me, like all those who love your name.

Command my steps according to your word, and don't let any iniquity have dominion over me. Deliver me from the false accusation of men, so I will keep your commandments. Make your face shine on your servant, and teach me your ordinances. My eyes have been bathed in streams of water because I did not follow your law. Righteous are you, Lord, and correct are your judgments. You have commanded righteousness and perfect truth as your testimonies. Your zeal has consumed me because my enemies have forgotten your words. Your word has been very fully tested, and your servant loves it.

I am young and despised, yet I have not forgotten your ordinances. Your righteousness is eternal righteousness, and your law is truth. Plagues and distresses found me, but your commandments were my meditation. Your testimonies are forever righteous. Instruct me, and I will live. I cried with my whole heart, "Hear me, Lord, and I will study your ordinances!"

I cried to you, "Save me, and I will keep your testimonies!"

I arose before the dawn, and cried, "I trusted in your words, my eyes preceded the dawn, so I might meditate on your oracles. Hear my voice, Lord, according to your mercy. Quicken me according to your judgment. They have drawn near, those who persecuted me unlawfully, and they are far removed from your law. You are near, Lord, and all your commandments are truth. I have known of old concerning your testimonies, that you have founded them forever.

See my affliction and rescue me, for I have not forgotten your law. Plead my cause, and ransom me. Quicken me because of your words. Salvation is far from sinners, for they have not studied your ordinances. Your mercies, Lord, are many. Quicken me according to your judgment. Many are those who persecute me and oppress me, but I have not declined from your testimonies. I saw men acting foolishly, and I pined away, for they did not follow your oracles.

Look, I have loved your commandments, Lord. Quicken me in your mercy. The beginning of your words is truth, and all the judgments of your righteousness endure forever. Princes persecuted me without a cause, but my heart was afraid because of your words. I will celebrate because of your oracles, like one who finds great wealth. I hate and abhor unrighteousness, but I love your law. Seven times in a day have I praised you because of the judgments of your righteousness. Great peace have those who love your law, and there is no stumbling block to them.

I waited for your salvation, Lord, and have loved your commandments. My mind has kept your testimonies and loved them greatly. I have kept your commandments and your testimonies, for all my ways are before you, Lord. Let my supplication come near before you, Lord, instruct me according to your oracle. Let my petition come in before you, Lord, deliver me according to your oracle. Let my lips speak a hymn when you will have taught me your ordinances. Let my tongue speak your oracles, for all your commandments are righteous.

Let your hand be prompt to save me, for I have chosen your commandments. I have longed after your salvation, Lord, and your law is my meditation. My mind will live and will praise you, and your judgments will help me. I have gone astray like a lost sheep, seek your servant, for I have not forgotten your commandments.

Psalms: Chapter 118 Notes

1 Codex Vacticanus: cyrie (ⲔⲨⲢⲓⲉ). Translation: sir (or lord)

- Dead Sea Scroll 4QPs^g: yhůh (𐤉𐤄𐤅𐤉)
- Aleppo Codex: yhůh (יהוה)
- Leningrad Codex: yehvah (יְהֹוָה)
- Targum to Psalms: yeyā (??)

As there is no evidence of Yhůh being in Psalms before Simon's Hebrew translation, the direct translation of Lord from cyrie (κύριε) is used.

Psalms: Chapter 119

A song of degrees.

In my affliction, I cried to the Lord, and he listened to me. Save my mind, Lord, from unjust lips, and a deceitful tongue. What should be given to you, and what should be added to you, for your cunning tongue? Sharpened weapons of the mighty, with coals of the desert. Woe to me, that my traveling is prolonged, and I have camped among the tents of Qedar.[1] My mind has long been a traveler, and I was peaceful among those who hated peace. When I spoke to them, they warred against me without a cause.

Psalms: Chapter 119 Notes

1 Codex Vacticanus: Kidar (ⲕⲏⲆⲁⲣ)

- Aleppo Codex: qdr (קדר)
- Leningrad Codex: kedar (קֵדָר)
- Targum to Psalms: ărābāê (עֲרָבָאֵי). Translation: Arabs

Qedar was a large kingdom in the interior of Arabia in the 8th through 4th centuries BC, which dates this psalm to that period.

Psalms: Chapter 120

A song of degrees.

I lifted my eyes to the mountains, from where my help would come. My help will come from the Lord, who made the sky and the earth. Don't let your foot be moved, and don't let your keeper slumber. Look, he that keeps Israel will not slumber nor sleep. The Lord will keep you. The Lord is your shelter on your right hand. The sun will not burn you by day, nor the moon by night. May the Lord save you from all evil. The Lord will keep your mind. The Lord will keep you coming in and you going out, from now and forever.

Psalms: Chapter 121

A song of degrees.

I was glad when they said to me, "Let's go into the temple of the Lord."

Our feet stood in your courts, Jerusalem. Jerusalem is built as a city whose fellowship is complete. For there the tribes went up, the tribes of the Lord, as a testimony for Israel, to give thanks to the name of the Lord. There are thrones set for judgment, thrones for the house of David. Pray now for the peace of Jerusalem, and let there be prosperity for those who love you. Let peace, I pray, be within your army, and prosperity in your palaces. For the sake of my brothers and my neighbors, I have indeed spoken peace concerning you. Because of the house of the Lord our god, I have diligently desired your good.

Psalms: Chapter 122

A song of degrees.

To you who live in the sky have I lifted my eyes. Look, as the eyes of servants are directed to the hands of their masters, and as the eyes of a slavegirl to the hands of her mistress, so our eyes are directed to the Lord our god until he has mercy on us. Pity us, Lord, have pity on us, for we are greatly filled with contempt. Yes, our minds have been greatly filled with it, we are the reproach of those who are at ease and contempt to the proud.

Psalms: Chapter 123

A song of degrees.

If it had not been that the Lord was among us, let Israel now say so. If it had not been that the Lord was among us when men rose against us, verily they would have swallowed us up alive when their anger was started against us, and verily the water would have drowned us, our mind would have gone under the torrent. Yes, our minds would have gone under the overwhelming water. Blessed is the Lord, who has not given us for a prey to their teeth. Our minds have been saved like a sparrow from the snare of the bird-catchers, the snare is broken, and we are delivered. Our help is in the name of the Lord, who made the sky and earth.

Psalms: Chapter 124

A song of degrees.

They who trust in the Lord will be like mount Zion. He who lives in Jerusalem will never be removed. The mountains are around her, and so the Lord is around his people, from now on and even forever. the Lord will not allow the wand of sinners to be on a lot of the righteous, and in case the righteous should stretch forth their hands to iniquity. Lord, do good to those who are good, and to those who are upright in heart. But those who turn aside to crooked ways, the Lord will lead away with the workers of iniquity.

Peace be on Israel.

Psalms: Chapter 125

A song of degrees.

When the Lord released the captives from Zion, we were the comforted ones. Then our mouths were filled with joy, and our tongues with celebration. Then they would say among the nations, "The Lord has done great things among them. The Lord has done great things for us, we become joyful. Lord, release our captivity, as the steams in the south. They who sow in tears will reap in joy."

They went on and wept as they threw their seeds, but they will certainly come with celebration, bringing their sheaves with them.

Psalms: Chapter 126

A song of degrees.

Unless the Lord builds the temple, those who build it labor in vain. Unless the Lord protects the city, the watchman watches in vain. It is vain for you to rise early. Rise up after resting, you who eat the bread of grief, and while he gives sleep to his beloved. See the inheritance of the Lord, children, the reward of the fruit of the womb. Like arrows in the hand of a mighty man, so are the children of those who were outcasts. Blessed is the man who will satisfy his desire with them, and they will not be ashamed when they speak to their enemies at the gates.

Psalms: Chapter 127

A song of degrees.

Blessed are all those who fear the Lord, and who walk in his ways. You will eat the fruits of the labors of your hands. Blessed are you, and it will be well with you. Your wife will be like a fruitful vine on the sides of your house. Your children like young olive plants around your table. Know, so will the man be blessed that fears the Lord. May the Lord bless you out of Zion, and may you see the prosperity of Jerusalem all the days of your life. May you see your grandchildren.

Peace be on Israel.

Psalms: Chapter 128

A song of degrees.

Many times they have warred against me from my youth, let Israel now say, "Many times have they warred against me from my youth, and yet they have not prevailed against me."

The sinners worked behind my back, and they prolonged their iniquity. Lord Sydyk[1] has cut asunder the necks of sinners. Let all who hate Zion be put to shame and turned back. Let them be like the grass of the housetops, which withers before it is plucked up. While the reaper does not fill his hand, nor he who makes up the sheaves, his chest, neither do those who go by say, "The blessing of the Lord be on you," and we have blessed you in the name of the Lord.

Psalms: Chapter 128 Notes

1 Codex Vacticanus: cyrios dicaeos (ΚΥΡΙΟCΔΙΚΔΙΟC). Translation: lord righteous

• The Great Psalms Scroll: ådny ṣdyq (צידק אגני). Translation: my Lord Sydyk

• Aleppo Codex: yhůh ṣdyq (יהוה צדיק). Translation: Yhůh Sydyk (righteous)

• Leningrad Codex: yehvah tzaddik (יְהֹוָה צַדִּיק). Translation: Yahveh righteous

• Targum to Psalms: yeyā zakkāâ (יְיָ זַכָּאָה). Translation: Yah victorious

The Great Psalms Scroll confirms that there were some Hebrew translations of Psalms that included the term Lord Sydyk as late as the Herodian Dynasty.

Psalms: Chapter 129

A song of degrees.

Out of the depths I have cried to you, Lord my Lord,[1] listen to my voice. Let your ears pay attention to the voice of my supplication.

If you, Lord, should mark iniquities, Lord, who will stand? For forgiveness is with you. For your name's sake I have waited for you, Lord, my mind has waited for your word. My mind has trusted in the Lord from the morning watch until night. Let Israel trust in the Lord, for mercy is with the Lord, and with him is plenteous redemption. He will redeem Israel from all his iniquities.

Psalms: Chapter 129 Notes

1 Codex Vacticanus: cyrie cyrie (ⲕⲩⲣⲓⲉⲕⲩⲣⲓⲉ). Translation: lord lord

• Aleppo Codex: yhůh ådny (יהוה אדני). Translation: Yhůh my lord

• Leningrad Codex: yehvah adonai (יְהֹוָה אֲדֹנָי). Translation: Yahveh my lord

• Sahidic Manuscripts: kêros (ⲕⲏⲣⲟⲥ). Translation: lord

• Targum to Psalms: yeyā yeyā (?? ??). Translation: Yah Yah

Psalms: Chapter 130

A song of degrees.

Lord, my heart is not praised, neither have my eyes been haughtily raised, neither have I exercised myself in great matters, nor in things too wonderful for me. I will have sinned if I have not been humiliated, but have celebrated my mind. Like the relation of a weaned child to his mother, so will you repay my mind. Let Israel hope in the Lord, from now on and forever.

Psalms: Chapter 131

A song of degrees.

Lord, remember David, and all his meekness, and how he swore to the Lord, and vowed to the god of Jacob, saying, "I will not go into the tabernacle of my house, and I will not go up to the couch of my bed. I will not give sleep to my eyes, nor slumber to my eyelids, nor rest to my temples until I find a place for the Lord, a tabernacle for the god of Jacob. Look, we heard of it in Ephrath, and we found it in the fields of the wood. Let's enter into his tabernacles, and let's worship at the place where his feet stood."

Rise, Lord, into your rest. You, and the ark of your holiness. Your priests will clothe themselves with righteousness, and your saints will celebrate. For the sake of your servant David don't turn away from the face of your anointed. The Lord swore in truth to David, and he will not annul it, saying, "Of the fruit of your body will I set a king on your throne. If your children will keep my covenant, and these my testimonies which I will teach them, their children also will sit on your throne forever."

The Lord has elected Zion, he has chosen her as a habitation for himself, saying, "This is my resting place forever, and I will live here, for I have chosen it. I will certainly bless her provisions, and I will satisfy her poor with bread. I will clothe her priests with salvation, and her saints will greatly celebrate. There will I cause to spring up a horn to David, and I have prepared a lamp for my anointed. His enemies will I clothe in shame, but on himself will my holiness flourish."

Psalms: Chapter 132

A song of degrees.

See now, what is as good, or what is so pleasant as for brothers to live together? It is as an ointment on the head that runs down to the beard, like on the beard of Aaron, that ran down to the fringe of his clothing? Like the dew of Hermon, that comes down on Mount Zion, for there, the Lord commanded the blessing, life forever.

Psalms: Chapter 133

A song of degrees.

Look now, bless the Lord and all the servants of the Lord who stand in the temple of the Lord, in the courts of the temple of our god. Lift your hands by night in the sanctuaries, and bless the Lord. May the Lord, who made the sky and earth, bless you out of Zion.

Psalms: Chapter 134

Alleluia!

Praise the name of the Lord! Praise the Lord, his servants who stand in the temple of the Lord, in the courts of the temple of our god. Praise the Lord, for the Lord is good. Sing praises to his name, for it is good. The Lord has chosen Jacob for himself, and Israel for his peculiar treasure. For I know that the Lord is great, and the Lord is above all gods. All that the Lord willed, he did in the sky, and on the earth, in the sea, and all depths. Who brings up clouds from the edges of the earth? He has made lightning for the rain, and he brings winds out of his treasures.

Who slaughtered the firstborn of Egypt, both man and beast? He sent signs and wonders among you, in Egypt, on Pharaoh, and all his servants. Who slaughtered many nations, and killed mighty kings, including Sihon king of the Amorites, and Og king of Bashan, and all the kingdoms of Canaan, and gave their land as an inheritance, an inheritance to Israel his people? Lord, your name endures forever, and your memory to all generations. The Lord will judge his people, and comfort himself concerning his servants.

The idols of the foreigners are silver and gold, the works of men's hands. They have a mouth, but they can't speak. They have eyes, but they can't see. They have ears, but they can't hear. There is no breath in their mouth. Let those who make them, be made like them, and all those who trust in them. House of Israel, bless the Lord! House of Aaron, bless the Lord! House of Levi, bless the Lord! You that fear the Lord, bless the Lord. Blessed in Zion is the Lord, who lives in Jerusalem.

Psalms: Chapter 135

Alleluia!

Give thanks to the Lord, for he is good, and his mercy endures forever. Give thanks to the god of the gods, for his mercy endures forever. Give thanks to the lord of the lords, for his mercy endures forever.

To him who alone has worked great wonders, for his mercy endures forever.

To him who made the sky through thought, his mercy endures forever.

To him who built the earth on the waters, his mercy endures forever.

To him who alone made great lights, for his mercy endures forever.

The sun rules by day, for his mercy endures forever.

The moon and the stars rule the night, for his mercy endures forever.

To he who slaughtered Egypt with their firstborn, for his mercy endures forever,

and brought Israel out from among them, for his mercy endures forever,

with a strong hand and a high arm, for his mercy endures forever.

To him who divided the Papyrus Sea into parts, for his mercy endures forever,

and brought Israel through the middle of it, for his mercy endures forever,

and overthrew Pharaoh and his army in the Papyrus Sea, for his mercy endures forever.

To him who led his people through the wilderness, for his mercy endures forever.

To him who slaughtered great kings, for his mercy endures forever,

and killed mighty kings, for his mercy endures forever,

Sihon king of the Amorites, for his mercy endures forever,

and Og king of Bashan, for his mercy endures forever,

and gave their land for an inheritance, for his mercy endures forever,

an inheritance to Israel his servant, for his mercy endures forever.

For the Lord remembered us in our low state, for his mercy endures forever, and redeemed us from our enemies, for his mercy endures forever.

Who gives food to all flesh, for his mercy endures forever.

Give thanks to the god of the sky, for his mercy endures forever.

Psalms: Chapter 136

For David. A psalm of Jeremiah.

By the rivers of Babylon, we sat and wept when we remembered Zion. We hung our musical instruments on the willows in the middle of it. For there they who had taken us captive asked of us the words of a song, and they who had carried us away asked for a hymn, saying, "Sing us one of the songs of Zion."

How should we sing the Lord's song in a strange land? If I forget you, Jerusalem, let my right hand forget its skill. May my tongue cling to my throat, if I do not remember you. If I don't prefer Jerusalem as the chief of my joy. Lord, remember the children of Edom in the day of Jerusalem, who said, "Raze it, raze it to its foundations!"

Wretched daughter of Babylon! Blessed will he be who will reward you as you have rewarded us. Blessed will he be who will seize and dash your infants against the rock.

Psalms: Chapter 137

A Psalm for David. By Haggai and Zachariah.

I will thank you, Lord, with my whole heart, and I will sing psalms to you before the messengers, for you have heard all the words of my mouth. I will worship towards your holy temple and give thanks to your name, on account of your mercy and your truth, for you have praised your holy name above everything. In whatever day I will call on you, hear me quickly, and you will provide me abundantly with your power in my mind. Let all the kings of the earth, Lord, give thanks to you, for they have heard all the words of your mouth.

Let them sing in the ways of the Lord, for the glory of the Lord is great. For the Lord is high, and yet considers the lowly, and he knows high things from far away. Though I should walk in the middle of affliction, you will quicken me, and you have stretched out your hands against the anger of my enemies, and your right hand has saved me. Lord, you will repay them on my behalf, and your mercy, Lord, endures forever. Don't overlook the works of your hands.

Psalms: Chapter 138

A psalm of David.

Lord, you have tested me, and known me. You know when I sit down and I rise. You understand my thoughts from far away. You have traced my path and my bed, and have foreseen all my ways. For there is no unrighteous word in my tongue. Look, Lord, you have known all things, the last and the first. You have fashioned me and laid your hand on me. The knowledge of you is too wonderful for me, and it is very difficult. I can't attain it. Where will I go from your spirit? To what place will I flee from my presence?

If I should go up to the sky, you are there. If I should go down to Sheol, you are present. If I take up the wings of Shahar[1] and camp on the other side of the sea, it would be vain as even there, your hand would guide me, and your right hand would hold me. When I said, "Certainly, the darkness will cover me. Even the night was light in my luxury."

For darkness will not be darkness with you, but night will be light as day. Darkness will be light to you. For you, Lord, have possessed my reins, and you have helped me from my mother's womb. I will give you thanks, for you are fearfully wondrous, and wondrous are your works, and my mind knows it well. My bones, which you made in secret were not hidden from you, nor my substance, in the lowest parts of the earth.

Your eyes saw my pure substance, and all men will be written in your book. They will be formed by day, though there should for a time be no one among them. But your friends, God, have been greatly honored by me. Their rule has been greatly strengthened. I will number them, and they will be multiplied beyond the sand. I awaken and am still with you. Oh that you would kill the wicked, God! Leave me, you men of blood. For you will say concerning their thought, that they will take your cities in vain. Have I not hated them, Lord, that hate you? Wasted away because of your enemies? I have hated them with perfect hatred, and they were counted as my enemies. Test me, God, and know my heart. Examine me, and know my paths, and see if there is any way of iniquity in me, and lead me in a correct way.

Psalms: Chapter 138 Notes

1 Codex Vacticanus: analabô tas pterygas mou cat orthon (ΑΝΑΛΑΒѡ ΤΑС ΠΤΕΡΥΓΑС ΜΟΥ ΚΑΤ ΟΡΘΟΝ). Translation: take up the feathers (or wings, sails, flippers) of mine towards (or during, into) upright (or right, true)

• Codex Sinaiticus: laboemi tas pterygas mou cat orthron (ΛΑΒΟΙΜΙΤΑСΠΤΕΡΥΓΑСΜΟΥΚΑΤΟΡΘΡΟΝ). Translation:

grasp (or receive, discover) the feathers (or wings, sails, flippers) of mine towards (or during, into) dawn (or dim morning twilight)

• Codex Alexandrinus: analabô tas pterygas mou cat orthron (ΑΝΑΛΑΒѠΤΑСΠΤΕΡΥΓΑСΜΟΥΚΑΤΟΡѲΡΟΝ). Translation: take up the feathers (or wings, sails, flippers) of mine towards (or during, into) dawn (or dim morning twilight)

• Septuagint manuscript 1219: analaboemi tas pterygas mou cat orthron (ΑΝΑΛΑΒΟΙΜΙ ΤΑС ΠΤΕΡΥΓΑС ΜΟΥ ΚΑΤ ΟΡѲΡΟΝ). Translation: take up the feathers (or wings, sails, flippers) of mine towards (or during, into) dawn (or dim morning twilight)

• Aleppo Codex: åšå knpy-šhr (אשא כנפי-שחר). Translation: I will carry the wings of Shahar (or dawn)

• Leningrad Codex: essa chanfei-shachar (אֶשָּׂא כַנְפֵי־שָׁחַר). Translation: I will carry the wings of Shahar (or dawn)

Šhr (𒀭𒌓𒁀) was the bronze age Canaanite god of the dawn, the equivalent of the Ancient Egyptian Khepri (𓆣), Sanskrit Ushas (उषस्), Avestan ušah (𐎢𐏁𐎰), Greek Êôs ('Ηώς), and Roman Aurora. The prophet Isaiah referred to Shahar as the father of Helel (later translated as Lucifer), suggesting that Shahar was still considered a god by the early Iron Age Israelites, before King Josiah's reforms. The word is not documented in Aramaic as the name of a god but simply means "dawn," explaining the Greek translation. As David is not otherwise described as having any sort of wings, the expression "wings of Shahar" is imported from the Masoretic texts.

Psalms: Chapter 139

A psalm of David.

Rescue me, Lord, from the evil man. Deliver me from the unjust man. Who has devised injustice in their hearts, all day they prepared for war. They have sharpened their tongue as the tongue of a serpent, and the poison of asps is under their lips.

Separate the psalm.

Keep me, Lord, from the hand of the sinner. Rescue me from unjust men, who intend to prevent my plans. The proud have hidden a snare for me, and have stretched out ropes as snares for my feet. They set a stumbling block for me near the path.

Separate the psalm.

I said to the Lord, "You are my God! Listen, Lord, to the voice of my supplication. God Lord, the strength of my salvation, you have screened my head on the day of battle. Don't deliver me, Lord, to the sinner, according to my desire. They have devised plans against me. Don't forget me, in case they should be praised.

Separate the psalm.

As for the heads of those who surround me, the plans of their lips will cover them. Coals of fire will fall onto the earth and on them, and you will throw down among them plagues. A talkative man will not prosper on the earth. Evils will hunt the unrighteous man to destruction. I know that the Lord will maintain the cause of the poor and the rights of the needy. Certainly the righteous will give thanks to your name, and the upright will live in your presence.

Psalms: Chapter 140

A Psalm of David.

Lord, I have cried to you, "Hear me, and listen to the voice of my supplication, when I cry to you. Let my prayer be set out before you as incense, and the lifting up of my hands as an evening sacrifice. Set a watch, Lord, on my mouth, and a fortified door around my lips. Don't incline my heart to evil things, to pretend pretenses in sins with those who work iniquity, and I will not. Don't let me unite with their chosen ones. The righteous will punish me with mercy, and reprove me, but don't let the oil of the sinner anoint my head, for my prayer will also be in their pleasures.

Their mighty ones have been swallowed up near the rock, and they will hear my words, for they are sweet. As a lump of earth is crushed on the ground, our bones have been scattered by the mouth of the grave. For my eyes are to you, Lord my Lord. I have trusted in you. Don't take away my life. Keep me from the trap which they have set for me, and from the stumbling blocks of those who work iniquity. Sinners will fall by their net, I alone will escape.

Psalms: Chapter 141

A Psalm of instruction for David, when he was in the cave. A prayer.

I cried to the Lord with my voice. With my voice, I made supplication to the Lord. I will pour out before him my supplication. I will declare before him my affliction. When my spirit was fainting within me, then you knew my paths, in the very way in which I was walking, they hid a snare for me. I looked on my right hand, and look, for there was none that noticed me. Refuge failed me, and none cared for my mind.

I cried to you, Lord, and said, "You are my hope, my portion in the land of the living. Listen to my prayer, for I have been brought very low. Deliver me from those who persecute me, for they are stronger than me. Bring my mind out of prison, that I may give thanks to your name, Lord, the righteous will wait for me until you repay me."

Psalms: Chapter 142

A Psalm of David, when his son pursued him.

Lord, listen to my prayer. Listen to my supplication in your truth. Hear me in your righteousness. Don't enter into judgment with your servant, for in your sight no living man will be justified. The enemy has persecuted my mind, and he has brought my life down to the ground. He has made me live in a dark place, like those who have been long dead. Therefore my spirit was grieved in me, and my heart was troubled within me. I remembered the days of old, and I meditated on all your actions. Yes, I meditated on the works of your hands. I spread out my hands to you, and my mind thirsts for you, like a desert.

Separate the psalm.

Hear me quickly, Lord. My spirit has failed. Don't turn away from me, or else I will be like those who go down to the pit. Cause me to hear your mercy in the morning, for I have trusted in you. Make known to me, Lord, how I should walk, for I have lifted my mind to you. Deliver me from my enemies, Lord. I have fled to you for refuge. Teach me to do your will, for you are my god. Your good spirit will guide me on the straight path. You will quicken me, Lord, for your name's sake. In your righteousness, you will bring my mind out of affliction. In your mercy, you will destroy my enemies and will destroy all those who afflict my mind, for I am your servant.

Psalms: Chapter 143

A psalm of David concerning Goliath.

Blessed is the Lord my god, who instructs my hands for battle, and my fingers for war. My mercy, my refuge, my helper, my deliverer, and my protector, in whom I have trusted. Who subdues my people under me? Lord, what is man, that you are made known to him? Or the son of man, that you take account of him? Man is like a vanity, his days pass as a shadow. Lord, lower your sky and come down, touch the mountains, and they will smoke. Send lightning, and you will scatter them. Send out your arrows, and you will discomfit them. Send out your hand from on high, rescue me, and deliver me out of many waters, out of the hand of foreign children whose mouth has spoken vanity, and their right hand is a right hand of iniquity.

God, I will sing a new song for you. I will play to you on a lute with ten strings. Even to him who gives victory to kings, who redeems his servant David from the hurtful sword. Deliver me, and rescue me from the hand of foreign children, whose mouth has spoken vanity, and their right hand is a right hand of iniquity, whose children are as plants, strengthened in their youth. Their daughters are beautiful, sumptuously adorned in the style of a temple. Their garners are full and bursting with one kind of store after another. Their sheep are prolific, multiplying in their streets. Their oxen are fat, and there is no hedge falling down, or crying in their homes. Men bless the people to whom this lot belongs, but blessed are the people whose god is the Lord.

Psalms: Chapter 144

David's psalm of praise.

I will praise you, my god, my king, and I will bless your name forever and ever. Every day will I bless you, and I will praise your name forever and ever. The Lord is great, and greatly to be praised, and there is no end to his greatness. Generation after generation will praise your works, and tell of your power. They will speak of the glorious majesty of your holiness and recount your wonders. They will speak of the power of your terrible acts and recount your greatness. They will speak the memory of the abundance of your goodness and will celebrate in your righteousness. The Lord is compassionate, merciful, patient, and abundant in mercy. The Lord is good to those who wait on him, and his compassion is over all his works.

Let all your works, Lord, give thanks to you and let your saints bless you. They will speak of the glory of your kingdom, and talk of your dominion, to make known to the sons of Adam your power, and the glorious majesty of your kingdom. Your kingdom is a kingdom of all ages, and your dominion endures in every generation. The Lord is faithful in his words and holy in all his works. The Lord supports all who are falling and sets up all who are broken down.

The eyes of all wait on you, and you give them their food in due season. You open your hands and fill every living thing with pleasure. The Lord is righteous in all his ways and holy in all his works. The Lord is near to all that call on him, to all that call on him in truth. He will perform the desire of those who fear him, and he will hear their supplication and save them. The Lord preserves all who love him, but all sinners he will annihilate. My mouth will speak the praise of the Lord, and let all flesh bless his holy name forever and ever.

Psalms: Chapter 145

Alleluia!

A psalm of Haggai and Zachariah.

My mind praises the Lord! While I live I will praise the Lord! I will sing praises to my god as long as I exist. Don't trust in princes, nor in the children of men, in whom there is no safety. His breath will go out, and he will return to the dirt, in that day, all his thoughts will perish. Blessed is he whose helper is the god of Jacob, who trusts in the Lord his god, who made the sky, earth, sea, and all things within them, who keeps truth forever, who executes justice for the wronged, who gives food to the hungry.

The Lord loosens the shackled ones. The Lord gives wisdom to the blind. The Lord sets up the broken down. The Lord loves the righteous. The Lord preserves the foreigner. He will relieve the orphan and widow, but will completely remove the way of sinners. The Lord will reign forever, your god, Zion, to all generations.

Psalms: Chapter 146

Alleluia!

A psalm of Haggai and Zachariah.

Praise the Lord, for melody, is a good thing. Let praise be sweetly sung to our god. The Lord builds up Jerusalem, and he will gather together the diaspora of Israel. He heals the brokenhearted and binds up their wounds. He calculates the multitudes of stars and calls them all by names. Great is the Lord. Great is his strength and his understanding is infinite. The Lord uplifts the meek but brings sinners down to the ground.

Begin the song with thanksgiving to the Lord, and sing praises on the harp to our god who covers the sky with clouds, who prepares rain for the earth, who causes grass to spring upon the mountains, and green plant for the service of men, and gives livestock their food, and to the young ravens that call on him. He will not take pleasure in the strength of a horse, and neither is he very pleased with the legs of a man. The Lord takes pleasure in those who fear him and in all that hope in his mercy.

Psalms: Chapter 147

Alleluia!

A psalm of Haggai and Zachariah.

Praise the Lord, Jerusalem! Praise your god, Zion! For he has strengthened the bars of your gates, and he has blessed your children within you. He makes your borders peaceful and fills you with the oil of wheat. He sends his oracle to the earth, and his word will run swiftly. He gives snow like wool, and he scatters the mist like ashes, throwing out his ice like morsels. Who will stand before his cold? He will send out his words and melt them. He will blow with his wind, and the waters will flow. He sends his word to Jacob, and his ordinances and judgments to Israel. He has not done so to every other nation, and he has not shown them his judgments.

Psalms: Chapter 148

Alleluia!

By Haggai and Zachariah.

Praise the Lord from the sky!

Praise him in the highest!

Praise you him, all his messengers.!

Praise you him, all his forces.

Praise him, Shemesh[1] and Yarikh.[2]

Praise him, all you stars and light.

Praise him, you sky above Shamayim, and the water that is above the sky.

Let them praise the name of the Lord, for he spoke, and they were made. He commanded, and they were created. He has established them forever, even forever and ever. He has made an ordinance, and it will not pass away.

Praise the Lord from the earth, you dragons, and all deeps, fire, hail, snow, ice, tempests, and the things that perform his word, mountains, hills, fruitful trees, cedars, wild beasts, livestock, reptiles, winged birds, kings of the earth and all peoples, princes and all judges in the earth, young men and virgins, old men with youths. Let them praise the name of the Lord, for his only name is praised.

His praise is greater than Eretz and Shamayim, and he will exalt the horn of his people, the praise of all his sacred ones, the Israelites, a people who approach him.

Psalms: Chapter 148 Notes

1 Codex Vacticanus: Hêlios (ΗΛΙΟϹ). Translation: Helios (or sun)

• Aleppo Codex: šmš (שמש). Translation: Shemesh (or sun)

• Leningrad Codex: shemesh (שֶׁמֶשׁ). Translation: Shemesh (or sun)

• Targum to Psalms: šimšā (שִׁמְשָׁא). Translation: sun

The worship of the sun god Shemesh was banned by King Josiah circa 625 BC, however, based on the writings of Baruch, the Judahites reverted to the worship of Shemesh after King Josiah was killed by Pharaoh Necho II. The lives of Haggai and Zachariah are dated to the Persian era.

2 Codex Vacticanus: Selênê (ϹΕΛΗΝΗ). Translation: Selene (or moon)

• Aleppo Codex: yrḥ (ירח). Translation: Yarikh (or moon)

• Leningrad Codex: yareach (יָרֵחַ). Translation: moon

• Targum to Psalms: sîhărā (סִיהֲרָא). Translation: moon

The worship of the moon god Yarikh was banned by king Josiah circa 625 BC, however, based on the writings of Baruch, the Judahites reverted to the worship of the old gods after King Josiah was killed by Pharaoh Necho II. The lives of Haggai and Zachariah are dated to the Persian era.

Psalms: Chapter 149

Alleluia!

Sing to the Lord a new song. His praise is in the assembly of the saints. Let Israel rejoice in him that made him, and let the children of Zion celebrate in their king. Let them praise his name and dance. Let them sing praises to him with timbrel and lute.

The Lord takes pleasure in his people and will praise the meek with salvation. The saints will rejoice in the glory and will celebrate on their beds. The exalting praises of God will be in their throat, and double-edged swords in their hands to execute vengeance on the nations, and punishments among the peoples, to bind their kings with shackles, and their nobles with iron manacles, and to execute on them the judgment inscribed. All his saints have this honor.

Psalms: Chapter 150

Alleluia!

Praise God in his holy places!

Praise him in the framework of his forces.

Praise him on account of his mighty acts.

Praise him according to his abundant greatness.

Praise him with the sound of a trumpet.

Praise him with lute and harp.

Praise him with timbrel and dance.

Praise him with stringed instruments and the organ.

Praise him with melodious cymbals.

Praise him with loud cymbals.

Let everything that has breath praise the Lord!

Psalms: Chapter 151

This Psalm is a genuine one of David, though super-numerary, composed when he fought in single combat with Goliath.

I was small among my brothers and youngest in my father's house, and I tended my father's sheep. My hands made a musical instrument, and my fingers tuned a lute. Who will tell my lord? The Lord himself, he hears. He sent out his messenger and took me from my father's sheep, and he anointed me with the oil of his anointing. My brothers were handsome and tall, but the Lord did not take pleasure in them. I went out to meet the Gentiles, and he cursed me by his idols, but I drew his sword and beheaded him, and removed reproach from the Israelites.

Prayer of Manasseh

Lord[1] almighty,[2] the god of our forefathers Abraham, Isaac, and Jacob and of their righteous decedents, he who has made the sky and the earth with all their adornment. He who has bound the sea with the word of your commandment. He who has closed the abyss[3] and sealed it with your fearful and glorious name. He whom all things revere and tremble before the face of your power because the magnificence of your glory is unendurable and irresistible the anger of your threatening against sinners. The mercy of your promise is both immeasurable and inscrutable, for you are the Highest,[4] compassionate, patient, and most merciful, forgiving of the evils of men. You, Lord, according to the abundance of your goodness, have proclaimed repentance and forgiveness to those that have sinned against you, and in the multitude of your kindnesses, you have decreed for sinners repentance to salvation.

Certainly, you, Lord the god of justice, have not appointed repentance for the just, for Abraham, Isaac, and Jacob who have not sinned against you, but you have appointed repentance for me a sinner. I have sinned more than the number of the sand of the sea. My transgressions are multiplied, Lord, they are multiplied, and I am not worthy to look at or see the height of the sky, for the multitude of my iniquities, being bowed down by many iron bonds, so that I can't lift up my head, and there is no release for me, because I have provoked your anger, and have done evil before you, not doing your will, nor keeping your commandments, but setting up abominations and multiplying offense.

Now, I bend the knee of my heart, begging your goodness. I have sinned, Lord, I have sinned, and I acknowledge my transgressions, but I pray and beg you, release me, Lord, release me, and destroy me not with my transgressions. Don't keep me in evil anger forever, nor condemn me to the lowest parts of the Earth, because you are God, the god of the repenting, and in me, you will show all your benevolence, so that I the unworthy, you will save in to your great mercy. I will praise you continually all the days of my life. All the forces of the skies sing to you, and yours is the glory forever and ever, Amen.[5]

Prayer of Manasseh Notes

1 Greek: cyrie (ΚΥΡΙΕ). Translation lord.

The books of Septuagint's Book of 4th Kingdoms, and Masoretic Kings, both clearly report that Manassah re-instituted Baalism in Judea when he became king, suggesting that this reference was to Ba'al. He is also known from Assyrian records and is, therefore, one of the few early kings of Judea that is attested by independent records. As Manasseh was considered one of the most 'evil' kings by the Levitical authors of 4th Kingdoms (Masoretic Kings), because he restored the land to Baalism, and restored the statue of Baal in the Temple of Solomon, it is likely that this prayer is to Ba'al, whose name means 'lord' in Canaanite as bôl (ᴸᴼᎶ), Aramaic as bôlå (ﬡ ᴸᵁᎶ), and Hebrew as ba'al (בַּעַל).

2 Greek: pantocratôr (ΠΑΝΤΟΚΡΑΤωΡ). Translations: almighty, all powerful

3 Greek: abysson (ΑΒΥϹϹΟΝ). Translation: abyss, another name for Tartarus (the Greek underworld)

The abyss is a common element in most ancient middle-eastern religions. In Egyptian beliefs, the abyss was called Nun (𓏌𓏌𓈖), meaning 'sky waters,' and like many of the other religions, this sea was seen as being a cosmic sea, both below the Earth, and above Sky, and reaching off to infinity. The cosmic sea was an early attempt to envision what is now called outer space, assumed to be composed of freshwater.

The Sumerian name for the primordial waters was ^{deity}Nammu (𒀭𒇉), however, they also referred to it as abzu (𒍪𒀊), meaning 'deep water,' and zuab (𒀊𒍪), meaning 'water deep.' The Greek name abyssou may have been derived from the Sumerian term abzu, however, does not appear to have been imported to Greek thought until the early iron age, as the word is not found in the Linear-B script of the Bronze age. The Akkadians called the Abyss tâmtu (𒋾𒊩𒆳), which meant 'lakes,' however, the god that lived in it was replaced with Ia (𒂊𒀀), whose name is believed to be derived from the Sumerian words 'praise' (𒇖) and 'water' (𒀀). The transliteration of the word as Ia is modern, and if transliterated in Akkadian, the name would have been Ṣēriš Muú, meaning 'praise water.'

Ea replaced the earlier Sumerian god ^{deity}Enki (𒀭𒂗𒆠), whose name translates as ^{deity}Lord Earth. During the Old Babylonian era, Ea was replaced by ^{deity}Nabu (𒀭𒀝), the ^{deity}Sun-calf ^{deity}Marduk's son, and the personification of the planet Mercury in Babylonian cosmology. In Babylonian cosmology, the deity of the Abyss tâmtu was ^{deity}Timimat (𒀭𒋾𒊩), generally transliterated into English a Tiamat.

Both tâmtu and Tiamat are recorded in Ugaritic as thm (𐎚𐎅𐎎) and Thmt (𐎚𐎅𐎎𐎚), indicating they were separate concepts in bronze age Canaan. In the book of Habakkuk, written around 612 BC, the goddess was referred to as Tehom (תְּהוֹם), presumably in Judahite, the precursor to Classical Hebrew which was written in the Canaanite script. By the era of Habakkuk, the Israelites had been living in Canaan for centuries, and the word yam (יָם) had replaced tehom as the word meaning seas. As Manasseh lived around 50 years before Habakkuk, his use of the word would have probably been the same as Habbakuk's, meaning that this was probably a reference to the cosmic sea, and not the seas.

4 Greek: ypsistos (ΥΨΙϹΤΟϹ). Translation: highest

The Highest is a reference to God, or a god, found in many ancient religions in the region. According to the Torah, the ancient people of Jerusalem worshiped El Elyon, which translates as Highest God when Abraham passed through the regions. The term Highest repeats through other early Akkadian Cuneiform, Canaanite, and Greek texts. The term ålhym (𐤓𐤆𐤀𐤋𐤗), and ålhym (𐤔^𐤍𐤋𐤍), were direct transcriptions of the Neo-Assyrian word elium (𒂊𒈗𒐐𒐖), which meant 'god.' During the bronze age, the same word, alium (𒂍𒐜𒐕𒐍), referred to a specific god: ^{deity}Ān (✳✳) the highest god, and father of the other gods. His Akkadian name was derived from the word elûm (𒂍𒐜𒐖), meaning 'higher,' as the term was intended to convey the meaning of 'highest.' He was believed to live in the polar region of the sky, where the modern constellation of Draco is located, making him the highest in the sky, around which all the gods (stars) circled.

5 Greek: amên (ΑΜΗΝ)

Septuagint Manuscripts

The following is a list of the Septuagint manuscripts referenced in the notes for this book.

LXX ℵ (Codex Sinaiticus) is dated to the 4th century. Sections are currently located at British Library (Add. 43725) in London, Leipzig University (Gr. 1) in Leipzig, National Library of Russia (Gr. 2, Gr. 259, Gr. 843, and Fonds. d. Ges. f. alte Lit. Oct 156) in St, Petersburg, and Saint Catherine's Monastery (МГ 1) on Mount Sinai.

LXX A (Codex Alexandrinus) is dated to the 5th century. It is currently located at the British Library (Royal 1 D. VIII) in London.

LXX B (Codex Vaticanus) is dated to the 4th century. It is currently located at the Vatican Library (Gr. 1209) in Vatican City.

LXX 55 is dated to the 10th century. It is currently located at the Vatican Library (Regin. Gr. 1) in Vatican City.

LXX 1219 is dated to the 4th or 5th century. It currently located at the Smithsonian Institution Libraries Freer Gallery (Inv. Nr. 06.273) in Washington.

LXX 1220 is dated to the 6th or 7th century. It currently located at the Austrian National Library (P. Vindob. K 9907-9971b) in Vienna.

Dead Sea Scrolls

The following is a list of the Dead Sea Scrolls mentioned in the notes for this book. Most are held by the Israel Museum in Jerusalem.

DSS 1Q10 (1QPs^a) is dated to the Roman Era in Judea (6 to 390 AD).

DSS 4Q83 (4QPs^a) is dated to the Hasmonean Dynasty in Judea (140 to 37 BC).

DSS 4Q84 (4QPs^b) is dated to the Herodian Dynasty in Judea (37 BC to 6 AD)

DSS 4Q85 (4QPs^c) is dated to the Herodian Dynasty in Judea (37 BC to 6 AD).

DSS 4Q86 (4QPs^d) is dated to the Hasmonean Dynasty in Judea (140 to 37 BC).

DSS 4Q87 (4QPs^e) is dated to the Herodian Dynasty in Judea (37 BC to 6 AD).

DSS 4Q88 (4QPs^f) is dated to the Hasmonean Dynasty in Judea (140 to 37 BC)

DSS 4Q89 (4QPs^g) is dated to the Herodian Dynasty in Judea (37 BC to 6 AD).

DSS 4Q90 (4QPs^h) is dated to the Herodian Dynasty in Judea (37 BC to 6 AD)

DSS 4Q92 (4QPs^k) is dated to the Hasmonean Dynasty in Judea (140 to 37 BC)

DSS 4Q94 (4QPs^m) is dated to the Herodian Dynasty in Judea (37 BC to 6 AD).

DSS 4Q96 (4QPs^{o}) is dated to the Herodian Dynasty in Judea (37 BC to 6 AD).

DSS 4Q98 (4QPs^{q}) is dated to the Herodian Dynasty in Judea (37 BC to 6 AD).

DSS 4Q98a (4QPs^{r}) is dated to the Herodian dynasty in Judea (37 BC to 6 AD).

DSS 5Q6 (5QPs) is dated to the Herodian dynasty in Judea (37 BC to 6 AD).

DSS 11Q5 (The Great Psalms Scroll / 11QPs^{a}) is dated to the Herodian dynasty in Judea (37 BC to 6 AD).

DSS 11Q7 (11QPs^{c}) is dated to the Herodian Dynasty in Judea (37 BC to 6 AD).

DSS 11Q8 (11QPs^{d}) dates to the Herodian Dynasty (37 BC to 6 AD).

DSS 11Q11 (Apocryphal Psalms / 11QapocrPs) dates to the Herodian Dynasty (37 BC to 6 AD).

DSS Masada Psalms^{a} (MasPs^{a}) is dated to the Roman rule of Judea (6 to 390 AD).

DSS Nahal Hever Psalms is dated to the Herodian Dynasty in Judea (37 BC to 6 AD).

DSS Apocryphal Psalms dates to the Herodian Dynasty (37 BC to 6 AD).

Also Available

ALSO AVAILABLE

ENOCH AND METATRON SERIES:
- Books of Enoch Collection

- Secrets of Enoch

- Books of Metatron Collection

- Books of Enoch and Metatron Collection

OTHER TRANSLATIONS:
- Apocalypses of Ezra

- Arabic Maccabees

- Hebrew Maccabees

- Life of Adam and Eve

- Memories of the New Kingdom

- Septuagint's Esther and the Vetus Latina Esther

- Septuagint's Ezekiel and the Ba'al Cycle

- Septuagint's Job and the Testament of Job

- Septuagint's Proverbs and the Wisdom of Amenemope

- Syriac Maccabees – Deuterocanonical Books

- The Amarna Letters

- Testaments of the Patriarchs Collection

- Tobit and Ahikar

- Ugaritic Texts: Ba'al Cycle

- Wisdom of Ahikar